Reflections on Becoming

Fifteen Literature-Based Units

for the Young Adolescent

by

Ronnie L. Sheppard

and

Beverly D. Stratton

NATIONAL MIDDLE SCHOOL ASSOCIATION

NATIONAL MIDDLE SCHOOL ASSOCIATION

Ronnie Sheppard, Chair of the Department of Middle Grades and Secondary Education at Georgia Southern University, is a former member of NMSA's Publications Committee and is the Editor of *Becoming,* the Georgia Middle School Association Journal.

Beverly Stratton, Chair of the Department of Early Childhood and Reading at Georgia Southern University, taught elementary grades five and six for many years in Ohio before joining the faculty at Georgia Southern in 1983 as a reading specialist.

Special thanks is extended to Donna Colson, Frances Keene, and Tina Southwell at Georgia Southern University for their work in the initial formatting of the manuscript, and to Mary Mitchell for her preparation of the monograph for printing.

Both the original art and cover design were created by Barbara Brannon.

ISBN: 1-56090-077-6

*To Katie, my wife and an eighth grade teacher, who provided
invaluable suggestions and reactions from the point of view of
a middle school teacher and who has always given me her
unlimited support and encouragement.*

Contents

Foreword

In Praise of Real Progressives

*What we have to do is separate the clowns and balloons from the
real progressives.*
                                                    —James A. Beane

Middle school education is a progressive education movement. Centered
around the concept of developmentally appropriate programs and practices for
young adolescents, it embodies progressive education with its focus upon
meaningful inquiry into life-connected topics through active student learning.

Reflections on Becoming: Fifteen Literature-Based Units for Young Adolescents is a
resource that embodies the progressive concepts of life-connected topics by
focusing on the search for self-understanding. Adolescent literature has historically evolved into a significant literature for youth. Like any category of good
literature it does not *tell*, it *shows*. And by showing adolescence as it is in the
nineties, it allows individuals to reflect upon their own development—physical,
intellectual, social, emotional, and moral.

But beyond showing aspects of development, adolescent literature does
something more profound for its readers. It tells the truth. And truth, for an
individual coming to grips with the savage inconsistencies of modern life, is a
rare commodity. *Reflections on Becoming* conveys this sense of truth-telling by
focusing on difficult topics that adults (parents, teachers, and the school's
curriculum) are often afraid to answer. This truth-telling is another indication
of the progressive nature of this work.

Reflections on Becoming will be useful to a range of audiences—classroom
teachers, librarians and counselors involved in teaching young adolescents,
preservice students engaged in understanding young adolescent development
or their literature, parents in search of directions to guide their child's reading,
and young adolescents themselves. Beyond the titles and topics that are offered
here, the authors provide their audience with a framework for involving young
adolescents in their own self-examination of becoming.

Ronnie Sheppard and Beverly Stratton have done a service to both teachers and youth in authoring *Reflections on Becoming*. But one would expect this kind of service from two progressive educators who make truth-telling a part of their individual teaching. These two educators, both university level department chairs, are exemplary teachers who convey their love for students, learning, and literature through their teaching. They approach their subject and their audience with respect, open minds, and an appreciation for the search for meaning that we are all about. They are, like middle school education and the book they have created, in the mainstream of progressive education.

Tom Dickinson, Editor
Middle School Journal

Introduction

"You mean you teach *fourteen year olds*?" Does this question sound familiar? If you are a middle school teacher, you more than likely have been asked this question, or a similar one, at some point in your career.

Even though the literature available on early adolescent development is readily available, the years between ten and fourteen continue to be a mystery to many. As the world has become more complex, the lives of young adolescents have become more of a challenge—to them and to the adults involved in their daily lives. New questions, new dilemmas, and new issues become common. Too often, these complexities are not yet understood by adults; thus children are left to cope with these conflicts on their own. Young people live in a world that is more and more confusing, thus the need to provide opportunities for young adolescents to reflect on these issues becomes even more significant in order for them to develop into functional adults.

Little attention has been given to experiences that would assist young adolescents in shaping a deeper understanding of their own development.

Children regularly confront situations that challenge their emotions and actions. Too often they are ill-equipped to handle these often complex situations. In many cases, they become frustrated as they attempt to make the appropriate decisions. Those around them may have superficial understandings of child growth and development; yet these understandings are in many cases merely surface understandings. The conflicts and concerns that face early adolescents are in most cases situational and can only be understood in the context in which they occur.

Middle level education continues to speak to the need for providing experiences for early adolescents that are developmentally appropriate. New school programs have been developed. New instructional strategies have been put into practice. Yet, little attention has been given to experiences that would assist young adolescents in shaping a deeper understanding of their own development. Growing up involves an active process of reflecting on one's own growth—physically, socially, emotionally, morally, and intellectually. Teacher-based advisory programs have made their mark in middle level education as an attempt to address these developmental features. In most cases these programs are discreet programs that become separate parts of the school day, with all too little connection to other parts of the curriculum. Evidence indicates that many of these programs have been very successful, yet many have not. They are often viewed by teachers and parents as unrelated to the main mission of the school, the academic program. In some cases, however, schools have integrated teacher-based advisory into the curriculum areas, thus attempting to merge academic and affective education for young people.

 *Opportunities for young people to respond to these books and make connections to their own development may provide the spark needed for them to confront their own development and accept their growth in a positive light.*

The need to provide school-directed opportunities for young adolescents to reflect on their own development is obvious. What is not so obvious are effective ways to accomplish this task. Understandings deepen as young people become engaged in their own life stories. Many of their stories are captured in the contemporary fiction that young adolescents read. These stories are mirrors to many of the concerns, questions, and dilemmas they experience. Characters in these stories confront those authentic experiences that focus on the changes they encounter, the struggles they face as they interact with their peers, and the fluid emotions that result as they attempt to cope with growing up. Opportunities for young people to respond to these books and make connections to their own development may provide the spark needed for them to confront their own development and accept their growth in a positive light.

The spirit of the monograph stems from the belief that young people learn best as they interact with their peers. Literature provides opportunities for young people to observe and vicariously live with characters acting and reacting to situations like ones they face. The classroom strategies described in this monograph are based on the conviction that early adolescent literature offers one avenue by which young adolescents can gain an understanding of the changes that occur as they move from childhood to full adolescence.

Understanding the 10-14 year old through early adolescent literature

Leigh Botts is a neat kid! He looks at life a little differently from most kids his age. At times, he thinks he is the only person who has any problems. He thinks about his parents' divorce. He wishes his dad would call. Yet, what his dad usually says is, "Well, keep your nose clean, kid." He wishes his dad would say, "I love you," and call him "Leigh" instead of "kid." Leigh wants what many young boys want—acceptance. Leigh is a fictional character created by Beverly Cleary in *Dear Mr. Henshaw,* yet Leigh is a boy like many of us know. He is intelligent; he dreams; at times he is mysterious; he has bouts of anger. He is what many call "troubled."

Leigh is one of many characters we get to know when we read early adolescent novels. He helps us feel, think, and wonder about those early adolescent years. Early adolescent books paint real stories about the conflicts that young adolescents face as they shape and reshape their world. Katherine Paterson's Jesse, for example, is a normal ten year old boy who has strong emotions and needs. Yet Katherine Paterson brings to us more than what is visible. We feel Jesse's desire to be accepted by his peers and family. We learn about his past and the reasons he acts as he does. We see the complexities of Jesse as we read the story and discover his frustrations.

Children's authors have no reason to present a distorted image of early adolescents. In fact, they are in many respects the most honest reporters of children and their lives.

Historically, children's stories have been stories that brought to us the adventures and innocence of childhood. However, since fiction changes as society changes, we now have early adolescent fiction that presents youth encountering the realities of the nineties. Authors are not psychologists. They are not educators in the traditional sense. They are not, many times, parents. They are people who draw on their surroundings to create stories that speak to us about human conditions. Children's authors have no reason to present a distorted image of early adolescents. In fact, they are in many respects the most honest "reporters of children and their lives." Early adolescent books bring to us stories about youth growing up in the city and their experiences living in a tenement house and playing in a crowded city park. Early adolescent books reveal those memorable moments that we wish, as adults, we had written down—those moments when we tried to convince our parents that we wanted our own room, moments in which grandpa came to live in the house and we had to cope with all the lectures about how we should behave, moments in which mom let us invite friends for a sleep-over when dad said no. Books help us remember such moments in our lives. For example, *Kelly's Creek* brings us a story about a boy who discovers a friend who helps him feel successful in a world that has labeled him "dumb." Judy Blume's *Blubbe*r helps us see that being overweight is not merely a physical concern for young people. It is an emotional and social dilemma. Margaret, in *Are You There God? It's Me, Margaret,* begins to think and reason as an adult. At first reading, one might respond, "Oh, Margaret is so mature for her age," yet she is a young girl who seeks answers to critical questions. These novels are difficult to categorize thematically. They are mirrors of the lives of young adolescents. Some might even conclude that they are not young adolescent novels at all, but are merely authentic stories about people, places, and events.

Some might even conclude that these books are not young adolescent novels at all, but are merely authentic stories about people, places, and events.

Unlike books about child growth and development, these novels focus on the stories in children's lives, rather than attempts to categorize their traits. Literature allows us to see children act and react as they encounter conflicts. Our understanding of children who have concerns about their physical appearance can be deepened as we read stories about children who worry about weight, height, or lack of coordination. We gain insights into children's attempts to make friends as we read books about children who struggle to be a part of a group at school, attempt to please both parents and friends, and attempt to make moral decisions.

The stories in early adolescent fiction frequently focus on situations that our young people understand. For example, conflicts may center around the loss of a parent and the reality that children may have to work in order to help support the family. Young adolescents are often put into predicaments that require them to fulfill both child and adult roles. In *Where the Lilies Bloom*, for example, Mary Call struggles between her desire to keep her dying father's promise to keep the family together and her own developing realization that she must help if she is to gain the knowledge she needs and increase the family's chances for survival. In *The Night Swimmers*, Betsy Byars creates a story about a girl whose mother has died. Living with her father who is more interested in his career than in the children, Rhetta attempts to be a mother to her two younger brothers. She learns to cook by watching TV commercials. She learns about how mothers act by watching mothers in the supermarket. Other stories focus on children and their need for friendships and security. The literature explores both the joys and sorrows of this unique relationship.

Contemporary multicultural literature portrays young people from all cultures as children who have common concerns.

In addition, books often deal with relationships with the elderly and the handicapped. The reality of physical changes in children are portrayed in Constance Greene's *The Ears of Louis* and *The Unmaking of Rabbit*. These stories show the fears children have about their appearance, such as when Louis responds to jeers of "Elephant Boy" and "Dumbo" or "Stay out of the wind or you will sail to Alaska." Books often take a look at children who strive to be individuals, children who survive unusual circumstances. With recent books, children from all backgrounds are represented. Inner-city reality becomes the focus in *The Planet of Junior Brown* by Virginia Hamilton, a moving story about living in crowded conditions and the discovery that one can find a place to be humane and develop relationships anywhere.

The emphasis on children from varied cultures has become a primary focus in many early adolescent books. Stories depict children realizing that they have roots in a rich cultural heritage. Only recently have we come to understand that books can also perpetuate a stereotype. Contemporary multicultural literature portrays young people from all cultures as children who have common concerns. The need to give and receive love, the problems experienced when children realize that the parents they love are getting a divorce, and fears associated with school achievement are universal and suggest that all children may have similar needs, fears, and problems. Virginia Hamilton's *Zeely* is a warm, sensitive story about an imaginative girl who makes a remarkable discovery about herself and others when she and her brother spend the summer on Uncle Ross's farm. She discovers the pride and sophistication of her uncle's neighbor, Miss Zeely Tayber. Books like Bette Greene's *Philip Hall Likes Me. I Reckon Maybe* and Mildred Taylor's *Roll of Thunder, Hear My Cry* present positive views about the black experiences. These books allow readers and children

5

opportunities to identify with others, extend their horizons, and gain personal insights into their own lives.

With new books being published yearly, the lens on young adolescents is being widened. Perhaps we need to take the advice of Judy Blume, whose daughter reads her manuscripts before she sends them to the publisher. Eudora Welty comments that her stories come from those we know—those people in the beauty shop, on the street, in their homes. Robert Burch has written about going to parties to watch people, listen, and draw from those experiences. Educators go to other educators, psychologists or adults for information about young people. Few go to children for information. Current early adolescent literature offers a context through which feelings, desires, and actions of youth can be examined, questions posed, and options considered for solving dilemmas that face early adolescents. The literature provides exciting events that stretch one's perception of growing up as a teenager.

Current early adolescent literature offers a context through which feelings, desires, and actions of youth can be examined, questions posed, and options considered for solving dilemmas that face early adolescents.

Moral issues surface in many of the books. Divorce, for example, can be devastating and confusing to young people as is witnessed in Peggy Mann's *My Dad Lives in a Downtown Hotel*. In Betsy Byar's *The Cybil War*, the conflict over what role to play in a school play may appear minor to an adult, yet seems to be a life or death situation to an early adolescent. The dangers of being young and naïve can be examined in *Getting Nowhere* by Constance Greene. We discover a young boy from a troubled home move from endless arguments with his parents to a boy stunned when his life was almost taken in an accident. Conflicts exist in books between young people and their desires and what adults expect of them. We all remember those stories that helped us understand human nature. Stephen Crane's *The Red Badge of Courage* left many people with a deeper understanding of the effects of war on youth, the struggle to survive, and the value of life. This phenomenon continues with stories about what is was like to be young and impressionable during the Civil Rights movement in a small South Georgia town. We learn what it was like to be young and an American-Japanese in California during the Pearl Harbor crisis. As the world changes, so do early adolescents. Alex Haley in *Roots* helped us hear stories from one generation to another. We see children growing up during the era of the jet plane and the H-bomb, and at the same time children who face new challenges such as attempts to control one's mortality as is experienced in *Tuck Everlasting*. The most trivial events to adults can become the most serious events to early adolescents. *Thirteen Ways to Sink a Sub* by Lois Lowry shows us the young student who schemes to find ways to get rid of a substitute teacher. Such a story reflects youth in the twentieth century. Literature also presents snapshots from the home that we all have witnessed: the time the family carved a jack-o'-lantern, the day mom cleaned her child's room as a reward for a good deed, and the day mom convinced dad to increase the allowance. Stories are like diaries in the lives of young adolescents.

Early adolescent fiction helps to enlarge our insights into children in the nineties in contrast to children prior to the sixties.

Early adolescent fiction helps to enlarge our insights into children in the nineties in contrast to children prior to the sixties. For example, Tom Sawyer and his boyish antics seem like light-years away. Prior to the sixties, books depicted families working together, the value of education, and well-defined roles played by males and females. Yet, after the sixties, books centered around early adolescents attempting to hold the family together, older children responsible for young children, and increased independence among youth. Books have become psychological studies of youth, relationships, and cultural differences. However, books remain only "case studies" of people. The meaning we draw from the stories lies in the reader. What is so powerful is the opportunity to use stories to question, ponder, clarify, and extend our understanding and percep-tions. How many of us have thought as we read *The Wizard of Oz* how it would feel to have one of the traits exhibited by the characters on their journey to Oz? How many of us saw manifested in these characters people in our own lives who exemplified these traits? How many of us when we read *The Diary of Anne Frank* wondered what it would be like to be that young, struggling to remain a child? Yet, our early adolescents are in many ways not so unlike Anne in her prison. The same fears, emotions, and dreams exist. Judy Blume once said that her stories evolve from her characters. The fourteen year old girl she writes about evolves from what fourteen year old girls do. Her skill as a writer lies in her skill in creating from reality young people who act and speak as young people. Her characters argue about concerns that young people have. The conflicts she creates are conflicts that are natural in the lives of young people. Her adult characters act as adults. What happens, as a result, is a story that comes alive, that lets us see these young people interacting with their surroundings. Becom-ing engaged in the stories in early adolescent books brings one face to face with those questions children ask, those feelings children have, and those dilemmas that children often encounter. Readers have often revealed that they read to be entertained, to be informed, to learn. If this principle is true, then books about early adolescents would do the same. Readers have often revealed that during the reading, they ask questions; they cry; they laugh; they yell; and they often reevaluate their own values and actions.

 *Becoming engaged in the stories in early adolescent books brings one face to face with those questions children ask, those feelings children have, and those dilemmas that children often encounter.*

The recent release of *Turning Points: Preparing American Youth for the 21st Century* (1989) by the Carnegie Corporation's Council on Adolescent Development urged us to take a closer look at our youth and our understanding of their development. An understanding of the nature of young adolescents is critical, yet often only assumed to be available to those involved in their education (Hillman, 1991). Young adolescents are engaged in situations for which they are poorly prepared and for which they have limited understanding. It is clear to many who work with young adolescents that they learn a great deal about themselves and others from the environments in which they act and react. As Arnold (1985, p. 14) pointed out, "Young adolescents are asking some of the most profound questions human beings can ever ask: Who am I? What can I be?" According to Beane (1990),

> . . . the issues that these questions imply focus on an understanding of the physical, intellectual, and socio-emotional changes that occur during this particular stage: developing a sense of personal identity, exploring questions of values, morals, and ethics to immediate and distant social relationships, finding a place of status in the peer group, developing a personally acceptable balance between independence from adult authority figures and continuing dependence on them for various kinds of security, negotiating the maze of multiple expectations in the home, the school, the peer group, and other settings of everyday life, developing a sense of self-worth, and others. School should focus on reflective thinking, identifying and judging the morality of critical ethics, problem solving, identifying and clarifying personal beliefs, evaluating personal aspirations and interests, social action skills, and searching for completeness and meaning in such areas as cultural diversity. (p. 37).

Developing positive attitudes toward early adolescents is best gained as we deepen our understanding and appreciation of them as individuals. This is especially true in fostering an appreciation of the heritage of the ethnic minorities, the children who have special needs, and the children who struggle more deeply during the growing up period. Becoming engaged in the lives of the characters in early adolescent fiction allows us to speculate about the "what if's" of children and their lives. The best way to understand our early adolescents is to observe and dialogue with our youth. Get to know them. Use any vehicle possible. Most of us have a surface understanding of the social, emotional, and physical traits of young adolescents, yet few of us have conceptualized these in the context of life's experiences. In part, one of the central problems of understanding youth is the attempt to separate this understanding from more global contexts: society, family, culture, economics, history, and other variables that make us what we are. It would be unheard of to study the habits of lions out of the context of the environment. Yet we attempt many times to study children out of the context of their interactions with their world. Literature presents this interaction to us to view, question, wonder, and contemplate.

Literature becomes a context through which we can view children. Actions of characters offer options for dealing with dilemmas. Characters give us deeper insight into the human condition.

Literature becomes a context through which we can view children. Characters in literature, unlike the lives of some children, experience situations from several viewpoints. Actions of characters offer options for dealing with dilemmas. Characters give us deeper insights into the human condition. For example, children witness jealousy when a close friend becomes a cheerleader or a new baby becomes a part of a family. Fear is witnessed when children move from one location to another or when a parent dies unexpectedly. Even a short separation from a parent may be the most feared experience for children. Children need to learn to deal with their emotions and develop ways to handle their feelings. Literature provides many examples of how young people handle problems. As observers, we gain a sense of how early adolescents often do not have the tools from which to draw realistic and workable solutions to these situations. For example, the story of a native American girl who longs for life among the wild horses in *The Girl Who Loved Wild Horses* by Paul Goble opens doors of discovery for adults and children.

The strength of literature as a window through which to understand children may be seen in Jean Fritz's *The Cabin Faced West*, a book that shows how a girl's love for her former home and way of life can cause her to be discontented with her new surrounds. Ten year old Ann does not understand why anyone would give up neighborhoods, school, and a church for a lot of uncleared land. Through the story, she looks longingly down the road toward her old home in Gettysburg, dreams about the excitement of her life here, and hopes that she will be able to return. The road becomes a symbol of her dreams. She remembers the glorious times her family had and decides that nothing is as beautiful as their new home and the rolling farmland cleared from the forest. Jean Fritz has developed a realistic story about a young girl facing and overcoming problems related to growing up and gaining new visions. Even though the book has a setting quite removed from children in 1993, the fears, emotions, desires, confusions, and longing have not changed. From the era of colonial America to Lawrence Yep's *Dragonwings* about a young Chinese American boy who must adjust to life outside his beloved Chinatown in San Francisco, young people bring with them those same concerns and fears. Those conflicting emotions that come with the confusion about being uprooted in the midst of changing bodies and attitudes continue to give us insights about young people growing up.

Conclusion

We often forget that we learned many of our beliefs about people and shaped many of our values by reading fairy tales, nursery rhymes, and the classics. Early stories brought to the people a picture of human weaknesses and needs. We were able to see ourselves through the actions and words of fictional characters. That activity has seemed to fade over the years. A central goal of the middle school is to provide classroom experiences that engage middle school students in reflecting on their own development. This monograph describes an approach that uses early adolescent literature as a vehicle for deepening children's understanding of their own development.

Involving early adolescents
in reflecting on their own development

Central to the development of early adolescents are opportunities for children to become engaged in meaningful school practices that acknowledge their needs and provide individual and social contexts through which to extend understandings of themselves. Early adolescent literature offers one opportunity for extending these understandings.

As one attempts to identify issues that are most critical to the development of young adolescents, the task becomes difficult. Children between the ages of ten and fourteen experience a wide range of rapid changes emotionally, socially, physically, and intellectually. Discrete categories in which to place these changes are difficult to identify. Literature on child growth and development seem, however, to place most developmental characteristics into two central categories: understanding self and understanding relationships. These two categories will serve as organizers for the strategies described in this section. Figure 1 illustrates the widening circle that reflects children's growth, moving from an understanding of self to an understanding of others and relationships with others.

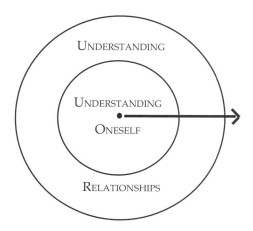

Figure 1: Areas for Self-Reflection

In order to reflect on these developmental features of young adolescents, themes have been identified in each area that reflect some of the central issues confronted by the ten to fourteen year old. These themes do not, in any way, portray a comprehensive view of the development of early adolescents; yet they do capitalize on some of the issues that seem to be of concern to young people. These themes will serve as organizers for the instructional units included in this section. Figure 2 illustrates these connections.

The central intent of this section is to provide opportunities for children to become engaged in activities that stimulate thinking about their own development. Units have been developed and organized around themes in Figure 2.

Each unit offers teachers opportunities to focus attention on the developmental characteristics of young adolescents by examining a character in a selected novel. The units are designed to engage students in large group and small group discussions or in journal writing about situations that are faced by young adolescents.

Figure 2: Themes for Classroom Units

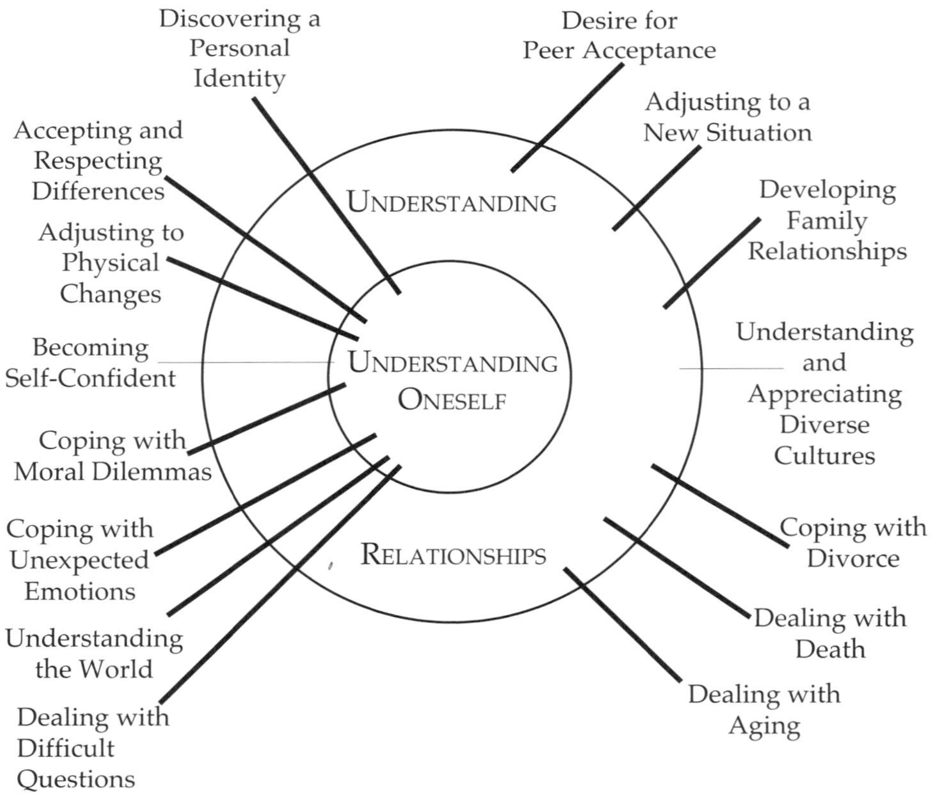

The units are built on three premises. (1) Children will become engaged in examining characters in fiction who face dilemmas that are authentic and real. By studying these characters, students will make connections between the conflicts faced by the characters and their own personal dilemmas. (2) Reflecting on these issues and dilemmas will personalize the stories and establish a bond between the characters and their dilemmas and their own personal questions and concerns. (3) Considering these situations will offer children an opportunity to consider how to address their own personal concerns in comparable situations. When children are able to relate the dilemmas to authentic situations, they begin to consider alternative actions.

Organization of the Literature Units

1. Case Studies: For each unit, a character in an early adolescent book has been identified who experiences some of the dilemmas faced by early adolescent children. The unit begins with a narrative case study of that character. These case studies provide a view of a young adolescent acting and reacting to a common conflict. The units in Area I focus on early adolescent characters attempting to *understand themselves.* The units in Area II focus on early adolescent characters who are engaged in *forming relationships.*

2. Accompanying Activities: Following each case study is a series of classroom activities that will engage students in reflecting on their own development. These activities are divided into three parts: (1) questions for discussion and / or journal writing, (2) exploration activities, and (3) a problem solving activity. Activities are intended to serve as sequential guides for using the case studies with middle school students. Figure 3 outlines the components in each unit.

As we examine the concerns of young adolescents, we gain a deeper sense of those individuals who will soon become our future citizens and leaders. In a world that is challenged by new thought, new values, and new knowledge, we dare not ignore the rich potential of youth. Young adolescents deserve the recognition they often demand. They exhibit those qualities that have been recognized for years as milestones in the lives of people. Their concerns are not always clear. What is often missing is the respect and recognition these concerns warrant. To explore them, young adolescents must become actively engaged in reflective thinking and problem solving. The avenues we take to provide those opportunities are only limited by the understandings we have of children and the fears we may have when we confront these concerns. Literature for early adolescents provides one avenue through which to stretch our thoughts and become more aware of how critical these concerns are in the lives of the ten to fourteen year old and also a means by which the young people themselves can understand the conflicts and problems inherent in growing up.

Figure 3: Unit Organization

CASE STUDY OF A SELECTED CHARACTER IN AN EARLY ADOLESCENT NOVEL

A narrative description of an early adolescent character dealing with a conflict. The case study may be read to the class, read in small groups, or read by individual students. Suggestions of additional literature that could be used to extend the unit are included.

ACCOMPANYING ACTIVITIES

A list of activities which will engage students in reflecting on their own development.

QUESTIONS FOR DISCUSSION AND/OR JOURNAL WRITING

Questions to stimulate thinking.

EXPLORATIONS

Activities to extend thinking and involve students in applying the concepts to their own development.

PROBLEM SOLVING

A problem solving activity that focuses on an authentic issue.

AREA 1
Understanding Oneself

Early adolescence is a period of development in which children attempt to develop their own identity, to understand the rapid changes that are taking place, and to experiment with a variety of behaviors and roles. With these changes come confusion, questions, and conflicts that are often misunderstood.

The need to understand these changes becomes critical to the development of individuals. The uncertainties that come with growing up are compounded as young people begin to experience rapid physical changes, new intellectual capabilities, and social encounters. As they interact with their surroundings, they begin to witness diverse views, inconsistencies in thought and behaviors, and more challenging expectations. To understand these changes is to understand the complexities of youth.

The complexities of these changes become more apparent as they surface in a wide range of contexts. For example, children become concerned that they are no longer going to excel in sports as they witness some rapid changes physically. Their desire to be the star of a football team may become shattered when they realize that their strength is not comparable with their peers. Such a situation is puzzling to the early adolescent. Their need to be accepted and recognized often depends on their ability to fulfill expectations of their peers and adults. Too often, their actions fall short of these expectations; thus they become confused.

Experience involving young adolescents in examining these changes and recognizing themselves as valuable individuals becomes critical during the early adolescent years. One of the central goals of Area I is to take a closer look at some of the recurring conflicts that early adolescents experience as they strive for their own identity. Each unit in this area focuses on selected conflicts that characters face as they search for an understanding of themselves.

Unit 1
Discovering A Personal Identity

Opportunities for young adolescents to reflect on their own personal identity are critical to the development of positive self-images.

During the early adolescent years, the search for self-understanding makes young adolescents vulnerable to external influences. They search for individual uniqueness yet desire to be a part of a social group. Young people begin to experiment with developing their own values, their own beliefs, and their own actions. This search to many young adolescents is frightening and riddled with risks. The desire to establish their own set of rules, and at the same time keep the links to the family in place, often results in erratic behaviors. Conflicts surface as they begin to receive mixed messages about what is acceptable. Early adolescents ask critical questions about sex, loyalty, physical appearance, language, and other dilemmas they experience. With this search often come disappointments as they test various behaviors in search of a personal identity and acceptance. Too often, children do not understand why they are unable to fulfill their own needs. Their attempts to be aggressive, form opinions, select their own interests, and respond to personal conflicts often lead to failure. They witness inconsistencies within their own peer group, as well as with adults around them.

A Case Study of Jesse

Bridge To Terabithia
by
Katherine Paterson

Jesse is in many ways a normal ten year old boy. He is a sandy haired, long-legged, fifth grader learning to deal with the emerging problems of adolescence. He comes from a rural Virginia area where most of the families are poor. This poverty, however, is not a real problem for Jesse as he says that "he didn't know people for whom money was not a problem." He has two older sisters and two younger sisters. He does most of the chores while the older girls are growing up, and he takes care of the younger ones.

In spite of his background, Jesse develops a social and emotional conscience. He seems to be aware of and responsive to the feelings of those around him. Jesse often does not like having these feelings, but they usually lead him to do the right thing. He has true empathy for others.

Jesse struggles with the personal needs of growing up as well as the pressures from his family situation. He loves his father dearly. He wants his dad to be proud of him, but his dad has a very parochial view of what is acceptable for a male child and of what a son should be. Jesse likes to draw. He says it "brings a peace that starts at your head and seeps all the way to your toes." When he was in the first grade, Jesse told his father he wanted to be an artist one day. His dad became angry that school was teaching his son this sort of thing. Ever since that day, Jesse has hidden his drawings from his dad. He sneaks up to his room and when others forget about him, he draws. Jesse is never satisfied with his drawings, but it is the only outlet for his feelings that he has, so he continues to draw.

The other children describe Jesse as "that crazy kid that draws all the time." Jesse seems to need to find that one thing about him this is unique, that thing that makes him special and accepted. One day during recess in the fourth grade, Jesse runs in the daily races and wins. For almost a day and a half, he is known as "the fastest boy in school." He was important. Jesse felt good about himself for the first time. He liked the feeling of success. Each morning he runs while the rest of the family sleeps. Finally on the first day of the new school year, Jesse loses a race to a new girl — Leslie—who has just moved in down the road.

At this point, Jesse really wants to dislike her. She robs him of the one thing he desires. But as Jesse mulls over his feelings, Jesse and Leslie become friends.

Leslie is different from the other children Jesse knows. She dresses, eats and acts differently. Her family is well off and has become "too hooked on money and success" and has moved to the country to "reassess their values." Her mother is a writer. Her dad writes and works in Washington D.C. Jesse wonders why everybody doesn't just accept these people and allow them to be different.

Leslie and Jesse find that outside their respective families, they share a great deal. As they play together, Jesse takes Leslie to a dried stream bed with a rope swing for crossing. As they cross and enter the woods on the other side, Leslie sees this as the perfect spot for them—a place so secret no one would ever know. They name the place "Terabithia." Leslie's imagination takes over. Leslie transports him into the imaginary land of Terabithia. It is the place where these two children escape throughout the story. Here, without the influence of adults and the preconceived ideas of others, they begin to grow and change. They begin to explore the feelings inside themselves. Using Leslie's vivid imagination and Jesse's growing wisdom, they create this mythical land and become its rulers. Leslie makes him king of Terabithia while she takes the role of queen. She shares with Jesse and in doing so gives back that special feeling she robbed from him that first day on the playground.

Ruling Terabithia helps them through the problems at school and at home. They learn to rely on this time to give them the support they do not find in the outside world. As they grow, they begin to take the qualities that they are forming in Terabithia into the real world with them. As a true king and queen, they acquire a sense of protectiveness toward others.

The time comes when, because of the weather, they cannot spend much time in their land. As the rain continues through several days, the water in the creek rises; and Jesse becomes scared each time they cross. He is determined to tell Leslie that he will not go again after the water recedes. But each day he puts it off. Before Jesse can face his fears of crossing the Bridge to Terabithia over the swollen creek and confronting Leslie, he is asked to spend the day with his music teacher. This teacher understands Jesse's love for the beauty in life and wants to help this passion grow. This is the most wondrous day Jesse has ever had. He feels guilty that he has not suggested that Leslie be invited, but he likes having this time to himself so he forgets about Leslie for a while. He returns home in a state of euphoria.

But Jesse has yet to face the greatest ordeal of his life. Leslie is dead. She has traveled to Terabithia alone while Jesse was on his outing. The rope used to cross to Terabithia becomes frayed and broken sending Leslie into the swollen waters of the creek below. Jesse must deal with the guilt of leaving Leslie behind and the loneliness of never being able to say good-bye to her. Leslie is not there to help him over this hurdle. She is no longer there to create the world of Terabithia. He has never been able to create Terabithia on his own, and he needs it desperately now. Jesse finally forces himself to cross the bridge alone and there in Terabithia says good-bye to Leslie in the way she would have liked. He lets the kingdom know that they no longer have a queen. He fashions a wreath of leaves and flowers and goes to the sacred woods to commend her spirit to God.

In honor of the queen, Jesse builds a true bridge to Terabithia to replace the broken rope. Through this action, he grows. Jesse truly becomes the king. As a true king, Jesse looks over his kingdom and realizes it needs a queen. So with maturity and understanding beyond his ten years, Jesse chooses someone who is worthy to one day be the queen of Terabithia and one who needs Terabithia to give her that special place to "become." Jesse realizes that what was important about their imaginary land was the things that Leslie gave him there —that sharing and chance to find one's self and a place to be special.

1. Who do you think knows you best? How does this make you feel?

2. What is special about you? What makes these features special?

3. What have you accomplished that caused others to be proud of you?

4. Is there anything about you that you feel is misunderstood by others? In what way? Why do you think they misunderstand you? How can you change this?

5. What opportunities do you have to be yourself? What would you like to be able to do that you have not had the chance to do?

6. What is one thing about you that you would like to change? How do you think you can make a change?

7. What have you learned over the past year about yourself or others that has helped you?

8. What emotions are difficult for you? How do you accept these emotions or deal with them?

9. What one personal quality do you feel you have because of the influence of someone you respect?

10. What do you think you will probably be like when you reach adulthood?

Related Early Adolescent Literature for Additional Case Studies

Vera and Bill Cleaver: *Queen of Hearts*

Jean Craighead George: *The Talking Earth*

Jean Craighead George: *My Side of the Mountain*

Jean Craighead George: *Julie of the Wolves*

Gary Paulson: *Hatchet*

EXPLORATIONS

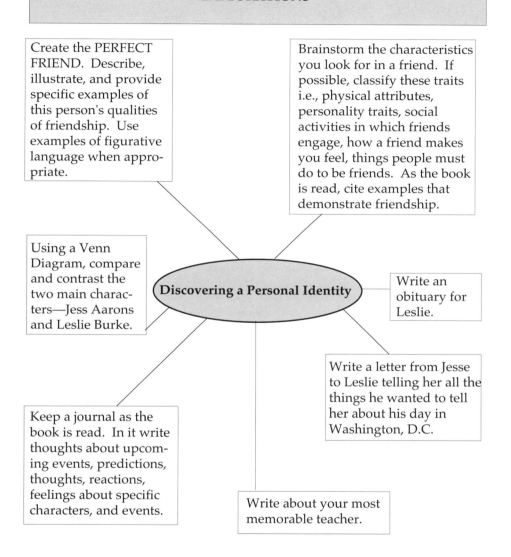

Create the PERFECT FRIEND. Describe, illustrate, and provide specific examples of this person's qualities of friendship. Use examples of figurative language when appropriate.

Brainstorm the characteristics you look for in a friend. If possible, classify these traits i.e., physical attributes, personality traits, social activities in which friends engage, how a friend makes you feel, things people must do to be friends. As the book is read, cite examples that demonstrate friendship.

Using a Venn Diagram, compare and contrast the two main characters—Jess Aarons and Leslie Burke.

Discovering a Personal Identity

Write an obituary for Leslie.

Write a letter from Jesse to Leslie telling her all the things he wanted to tell her about his day in Washington, D.C.

Keep a journal as the book is read. In it write thoughts about upcoming events, predictions, thoughts, reactions, feelings about specific characters, and events.

Write about your most memorable teacher.

PROBLEM SOLVING

If you could change your school to provide more opportunities for you to use your talents or interests, what school activities would you recommend?

Unit 2
Accepting and Respecting Differences

Understanding diversity, both the conflicts that come with diversity as well as the richness in diversity, is central to one's respect of others.

Early adolescence is a time in which children become aware that relationships with others may not be what they thought. With the need for developing relationships, they often witness inconsistencies among people. They see inconsistencies that are confusing, especially in a world in which diversity has become more common. Myths about differences exist that often cause young adolescents to form relationships and perceptions of self and others based on false information brought to them from the home, friends, school, and media.

In a world that has become more diverse, young adolescents in the nineties find themselves engaged in situations that they do not understand. A positive concept of self relies heavily on a respect of others and their individual differences. What comes with early adolescence is the realization that life is not simple, that what they may have experienced in their youth is not what they will witness as they encounter new experiences. Their experiences as they cope with changes and diversity are compounded during a time in which they develop abilities to note differences. Often, their ability to handle abstraction collides with their literal interpretation of the world. New adventures and challenges are scary for them. Questions surface as they come in contact with these changes and differences. Such experiences not only help to build healthy relationships, but also clarify who they are and help build a respect for their own individual differences.

A Case Study of Kelly

Kelly's Creek
by
Doris Buchanan Smith

Nine year old Kelly O'Brien lives in Brunswick, Georgia with his mother, father, and sister. Their house sits on a bluff overlooking the marsh. Behind the house, there is a runlet that connects Kelly's backyard to the creek. The creek is Kelly's favorite place to be. Each day after school, Kelly can hardly wait to get to the creek. He has recently met Phillip from Brunswick Junior College who is doing a study of marine life in the marsh. Phillip has taught Kelly all about the creatures there. Kelly knows that when he is in the marsh, he feels smart.

The portrait Doris Buchanan Smith paints of Kelly is that of a kid who tries desperately to be successful. However, the conflict in the story is that Kelly's physical, intellectual, emotional, and social abilities are limited because of a learning disability. He has a visual perception problem which he does not understand. The doctor says it is his eyes. Therefore, Kelly wonders why he does not have glasses. He cannot read, write, or ride a bicycle. Kelly sees himself as dumb because he cannot run and think at the same time. When Kelly is hurting inside, he forces a grin to cover his feelings and pain.

Kelly is in a special education class part of the day. When he is in class, he has a problem sitting still. Being still sometimes takes all his energy. There was one particular day he had to force himself to be still. When his arm kept moving across his desktop, he said to his arm, "Be still. You will get me in trouble." Kelly was already in plenty of trouble. His last progress report had shown no progress. His parents restricted him from visiting the creek. After this, his teachers sent daily reports to his parents. Kelly's learning exercises include templates of a circle, triangle, and square of which he traces the shapes with his finger. These exercises help his brain and hands learn to work together.

His friend, Phillip, is Kelly's only real friend. It is Phillip who convinces Kelly's mother that Kelly should tell his class about the marsh. Kelly does, and he is brilliant. He knows more about the marsh than anyone in his classroom. After this, Kelly's daily reports begin to show improvement. Slowly, Kelly gains confidence in himself. He begins to gain the confidence he needs.

1. Tell or write about a time you felt inadequate because you were different from someone else? How did you feel? Why did you feel that way?

2. In what way do you feel that individuals your age are misunderstood? How can you help others get to know you better?

3. Why are individuals not accepted sometimes because they are different? Is there a way to be accepted even if you are different?

4. What does "special" mean? Are there individuals you know who have qualities that make them special? Should they be viewed or treated differently from others?

5. How have you helped someone overcome a personal conflict? How did you feel?

6. If you could change yourself, what would you change?

7. Describe a time in which being different from someone pleased you? In what way?

8. Describe people who are different from you. How are they different, and why do you admire them?

9. How are you different from your parents? Your teacher?

10. What are some differences about others that you do not understand?

Related Early Adolescent Literature for Additional Case Studies

Judy Blume: *Deenie*

Julia Cunningham: *Burnish Me Bright*

Virginia Hamilton: *Zeely*

Vera and Bill Cleaver: *Me Too*

Create a cartoon that includes characters who are different but learn something from each other.

Demonstrate a talent or skill that you have that others cannot do.

Design posters that spotlight someone different.

Accepting and Respecting Differences

Design school activities that you could do to assist those with handicaps or special needs.

Research a person who is different from you, from a different place, or different time. Which would you rather be?

Interview others to discover how they are different from you. What did you learn?

PROBLEM SOLVING

Compose a "brag page" celebrating your special accomplishments or the accomplishments of someone else.

Unit 3
Becoming Self-Confident

Gaining self-confidence is a process of discovering one's potential.

A time of change is difficult. Having a positive sense of self that provides a foundation for approaching new tasks, adjusting to changes, or dealing with new decisions provide individuals the strength with which to cope. Yet, during the early adolescent years, feelings of inadequacies increase. Social encounters, academic expectations, adjustments to change in the family, and changes in physical characteristics bring a unique set of feelings and emotions. Yet, early adolescents often expect the worst. Their experiences with handling these new experiences are often minimal, thus they feel failure. Their self-confidence determines how successful they will be in handling these changes. The shaping of a strong self-image and the confidence to face new challenges become central to growing up during the early adolescent years. The need to discover that they have the skills to be successful and to be a contributing individual is crucial. Providing experiences that will engage young adolescents in discovering that risk-taking is part of growing up should become a central part of their lives. Knowing that new experiences can be rewarding and safe allows young people to accept new responsibilities and gain a sense of self-control.

A Case Study of Jamie

Come Sing, Jimmy Jo
by
Katherine Paterson

Jamie, a gifted eleven year old boy exhibits what many young boys face as they attempt to identify their place in the world and overcome some of the inner conflicts that come with shyness and a lack of self-confidence. Jamie's fears materialize after he joins his Appalachian family's musical group and moves away from his home and his grandmother. Jamie experiences for the first time the perils of independence when he leaves a warm, secure environment of his grandmother for the excitement and often unexpected events of a new place. Jamie's confidence in himself as a singer causes frustration and fear of being a failure. No longer is he able to rely on a confirmation of his worth among his relatives. He is on his own. His lack of understanding of other people influence his confidence. He does not know what to expect.

As his attitudes toward his talents in music become more positive and after he proves to himself that he is talented, his responses change toward his audience. He changes from being a frightened, distant individual to a social being. The tension he felt often caused him to become nauseated when he played in front of a group of people. He relies heavily on the belief that his father, not his mother, would protect him from the excited and aggressive fans. Through his confidence, he comes to realize that he is truly talented and discovers a personal satisfaction in sharing his talent with others.

Jamie, like many early adolescents, moves from an individual who holds on to what is known and secure to an acceptance of new challenges. The situation, however, is not an easy one. His fear of the unexpected changes. Jamie grows emotionally as he interacts with others.

1. What do you feel you can do that very few people know about?

2. What do you fear about new tasks or activities that you do not know how to do? How do others help you become successful?

3. Have you every been asked to do something that you were not sure you could do? What did you do?

4. How can you help someone learn how to do a new task?

5. Who helps you accomplish a task that is new to you? How do they help you?

6. What are some qualities you have that you want to keep?

7. Do you think you can accomplish most tasks if you try or if others help you? Describe a time when this happened.

8. How can making mistakes help you? Describe a time when this was true.

9. What changes are needed in school in order to help you be more success-ful?

10. What do you now know that you think you will probably learn with more time?

Related Early Adolescent Literature for
Additional Case Studies

Doris Buchanan Smith: *Kelly's Creek*

Mildred Taylor: *Roll of Thunder, Hear My Cry*

Judy Blume: *Blubber*

Lois Lowry: *What Do You Do When Your Mouth Won't Open?*

Paula Fox: *One-Eyed Cat*

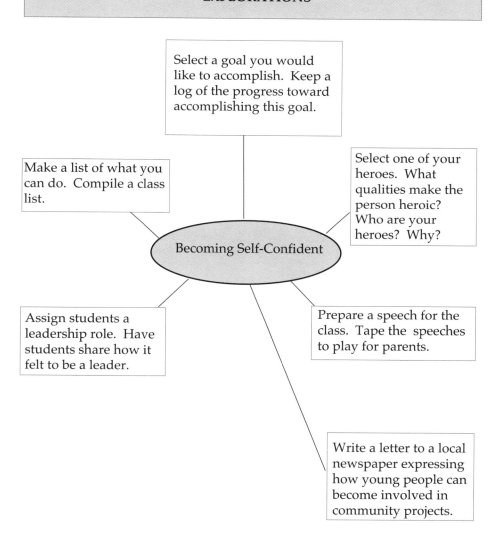

Select a goal you would like to accomplish. Keep a log of the progress toward accomplishing this goal.

Make a list of what you can do. Compile a class list.

Select one of your heroes. What qualities make the person heroic? Who are your heroes? Why?

Becoming Self-Confident

Assign students a leadership role. Have students share how it felt to be a leader.

Prepare a speech for the class. Tape the speeches to play for parents.

Write a letter to a local newspaper expressing how young people can become involved in community projects.

PROBLEM SOLVING
You are in charge of a community project. Plan the project. Outline your responsibilities. How will you determine if the project is a success?

Unit 4
Adjusting to Physical Changes

Respect of one's changing self is vital for a healthy, productive life.

Rapid physical changes during the early adolescent years may seem obvious and trivial. To middle school students, the changes bring with them major concerns and questions. These changes will have an impact on what the individual will be, believe, and feel about self and others. Acceptance of self and others is often difficult for middle school students. At a time when socialization becomes central, when values are being shaped, when challenges are confronting them, middle school students become preoccupied with their appearance. New fears evolve. New perceptions of others evolve. If these changes are not addressed, false assumptions may be formed about themselves and others. Not only is appearance critical, but many children do not understand how changes in the body are causing other changes, such as attitudes or feelings. The need to help young adolescents understand these changes, cope with these changes, and channel their lives in directions that take into account these changes becomes critical. Too often, behaviors are blamed on social, emotional, and intellectual issues, when in reality they may stem from physical changes. As has been stated in *Turning Points: Preparing American Youth for the 21st Century* (1989) and Elkind's *The Hurried Child* (1981), we must face these situations and provide an education for children that will help them accept these changes as normal if they are to become healthy, responsible, secure individuals.

A Case Study of Jill and Linda

Blubber
by
Judy Blume

Jill Brenner is a fifth grade student in Mrs. Minish's class. She is an avid stamp collector, loves to tease her younger brother (Kenny), is trying to let her nails grow (not bite them), and sometimes has to sit on her hands to "keep from doing it," loves to dress up and go trick-or-treating for Halloween, plays poker with her family and is "careful not to give my hand away by the expression on my face." All in all, a rather typical ten year old!

In Mrs. Minish's fifth grade, each of the students gives an oral report on an animal. During these reports, some of the students "look at" *National Geographic* or play tic-tac-toe instead of listening. Mrs. Minish sometimes keeps "her eyes closed for longer than a blink" and at the conclusion of each report says, "Very nice, (name of individual student)." Linda Fischer's report is on the whale. During Linda's report, Wendy passes a note to Caroline. It says, "Blubber is a good name for her." That's how Linda gets her nickname and the book gets its title.

Wendy, Caroline, and most of the other fifth graders call Linda names, tease, and taunt her. They harass her in the Girls' Room. They "roll" her house on Halloween. They play keep-away with her jacket, her Hostess cupcake, and her shiny red apple. They compose a "How to Have Fun with Blubber" list. Their antics illustrate how obnoxious some fifth graders can be to each other and to adults.

It is finally decided that Linda should have a trial. "Just like in real life with a judge and a jury and everything." Everything is set until Rochelle, who never says anything, brings up a point of law—"Every trial has two lawyers . . . one for the defense and one for the prosecution." Blubber needs a lawyer in order to "do it right." The subsequent confrontation between Jill and Wendy makes Jill realize, "For the first time I looked right into Wendy's eyes and I didn't like what I saw." When Wendy is instrumental in turning the class against Jill (BB = Baby Brenner), Jill experiences the full reality of how "rough it is to be on the other side."

1. What physical changes have taken place that are not pleasant?

2. What are some physical traits you would like to have that you do not have now?

3. What do you feel you could do to assure that you become a healthy individual?

4. What problems usually exist because of a physical trait individuals your age have?

5. There are people with physical disabilities who have established their own identity. Who were some of these individuals? How did they cope with their physical disabilities?

6. What have you experienced in school or at home that have caused problems because of a physical feature?

7. What questions do you have about physical changes that would help explain what is happening to you?

8. What do you think others expect of you physically?

9. How do you think you will change physically in the future? Why?

10. What are some facts about physical changes that should be understood by individuals your age? By adults?

Related Early Adolescent Literature For Additional Case Studies

Constance Greene: *The Unmaking of Rabbitt*

Constance Greene: *The Ears of Louis*

Judy Blume: *Are You There God? It's Me, Margaret.*

Judy Blume: *Then Again, Maybe I Won't*

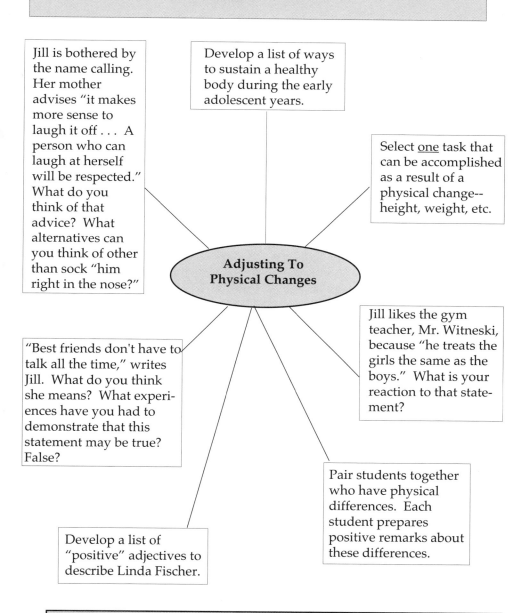

Jill is bothered by the name calling. Her mother advises "it makes more sense to laugh it off . . . A person who can laugh at herself will be respected." What do you think of that advice? What alternatives can you think of other than sock "him right in the nose?"

Develop a list of ways to sustain a healthy body during the early adolescent years.

Select <u>one</u> task that can be accomplished as a result of a physical change-- height, weight, etc.

Adjusting To Physical Changes

Jill likes the gym teacher, Mr. Witneski, because "he treats the girls the same as the boys." What is your reaction to that statement?

"Best friends don't have to talk all the time," writes Jill. What do you think she means? What experiences have you had to demonstrate that this statement may be true? False?

Pair students together who have physical differences. Each student prepares positive remarks about these differences.

Develop a list of "positive" adjectives to describe Linda Fischer.

PROBLEM SOLVING

Develop some school or community activities that would be ways to involve all individuals your age regardless of their physical appearance and capabilities.

Unit 5
Coping With Moral Dilemmas

In order to meet the demands of a changing and more complex society, our youth need to confront more challenging moral issues.

Growing up brings with it added responsibilities, especially as early adolescents begin to develop their own views and beliefs. Experiences become tangled as they experience multiple viewpoints that challenge their decisions. Their vulnerability leads to confusion, questions, and disappointments, especially about ethical issues. Situations that were once taken for granted become moral issues in the minds of young people, yet limited experience may prevent them from making decisions and facing consequences for their actions. Too often, they are placed in situations in which they have to act alone, thus creating new problems when they are not equipped to make these decisions. Too, they begin to see inconsistencies in how others react. No longer do they trust what they see adults do. They see inconsistencies and actions that contradict what they were taught as right and wrong. They begin to challenge adults' views. They rely often on what is acceptable with those whom they are interacting at the time. Yet this, too, brings frustrations when they do not see these decisions as being helpful to them. As a result, they often flounder.

During the early adolescent years, the many decisions and challenges they face often become paramount and difficult to sort into meaningful categories. They act many times on impulse. They avoid making some decisions in hopes that the difficulties will go away. The middle level years, however, are ones in which values are being shaped, actions are being refined and expanded, and new thought processes are evolving. The time is ripe for middle graders to become engaged in moral issues, in making decisions, and in looking at these issues from varied points of view. As is pointed out in *Turning Points: Preparing American Youth for the 21st Century* (1989), our youth are now faced with more and more critical issues concerning health, relationships, and values. In order to meet the demands of a changing and more complex society, they need to have experience in dealing with global issues. Positive self-concepts and relationships with people are built on interactions that involve decision making and are positive and supportive.

A Case Study of Ned

One-Eyed Cat
by
Paula Fox

The story of Ned provides a strong illustration of a situation in which one becomes engaged in a moral dilemma that changes one's life. Ned's Uncle Hilary gives him a loaded air rifle for his eleventh birthday. Yet, Ned's father, like many fathers, does not feel that Ned should have a loaded gun. His rule is not to use the gun until he is fourteen. Ned's father proceeds to hide the gun in the attic.

Ned's personality evolves as he experiences a struggle between what he feels he is capable of doing, his view of himself as a growing individual who should be granted more responsibility, and the demands of his father. Ned does not always trust his father. In fact, he feels that his father should not trust him and put the gun in a place that is fully accessible. Ned does not know why his father trusts him, since he does not trust his father. This situation becomes a game of "fairness."

The conflict mushrooms when Ned violates his father's rule by taking the gun. Ned accidentally shoots a stray cat and becomes distraught when he thinks about what happened. He becomes afraid and for the first time begins to feel strong feelings of guilt. This is amplified when he notices the wound—the dried blood, the mucus from the cat's eye that had been destroyed in the shooting.

A change in Ned occurs when he becomes overly protective of the one-eyed cat during the winter months. He feels a strong need to protect the animal from sickness and starvation. His sense of guilt at what had happened increases. He ponders what to do—torn between keeping silent about the incident and telling the truth.

His life begins to turn around when he confesses to an elderly neighbor what had happened. Even so, he still feels guilty. His relief comes when he finally confesses to his mother when they see the one-eyed cat come from the woods. Like many young people, Ned struggles between confessing and facing the consequences or keeping the story to himself and being miserable.

1. Have you ever been in a position in which you were pressured to do something that you knew was wrong? How did you deal with this dilemma?

2. What are some situations among individuals your age that lead to making decisions about whether to do what your friends do as opposed to what others expect you to do? How do you deal with these conflicting expectations?

3. What helps you determine what is "right" and what is "wrong?" Who helps you make these decisions?

4. What do you feel are some workable strategies to employ when you are presented with a choice that may not be acceptable by others?

5. Are there actions you see adults do that confuse you about what is "right" and is "wrong?" What confuses you?

6. What are some actions you do consistently that are right?

7. How old should young people be before they should be expected to make their own decisions?

8. What kinds of decisions are the most difficult for you? How do you deal with these?

9. What is more difficult—pleasing your friends or pleasing adults? Why?

10. Have you ever been put in a position to change your mind about an action? Did you make the right decision?

Related Early Adolescent Literature for
Additional Case Studies

Norma Klein: *Mom, the Wolfman and Me*

Lois Duncan: *Killing Mr. Griffin*

Bette Greene: *Summer of My German Soldier*

Judy Blume: *Then Again, Maybe I Won't*

EXPLORATIONS

Look through the newspaper to come up with a list of situations in which people make wrong decisions or act without careful thought.

Select one situation in which a decision that is made could lead to a problem in your life. Plan three strategies that you feel you could do to prevent this from taking place.

Compose a *Dear Abby* column that poses a dilemma and respond as if you were Abby.

Coping with Moral Dilemmas

Design a code of ethics for a "winner" and a "loser."

Design a slogan or short message to encourage others your age how to be more responsible in their actions.

Interview other students in the school to determine what they view as the most difficult decisions to make.

PROBLEM SOLVING
You are in charge of designing a campaign or advertisement for a local TV show to try to convince people your age to think about consequences before they get involved in activities that may be unacceptable or harmful. Design a skit, series of slogans, or ads that you feel would appeal to your peers.

Unit 6
Coping With Unexpected Emotions

An examination of the changing emotions of young adolescents serves as a window to the excitement, as well as the frustrations, of growing up.

To understand early adolescents is to understand the complexities of feelings and emotions of children as they confront both the pains and joys of growing up. Emotions are unpredictable. They surface in many forms. They are often puzzling to those around them. As children attempt to make meaning out of their lives, develop new friends, and cope with changing bodies, many of the reactions to these come in the form of highs and lows in the feelings and attitudes of our young people. These unexpected shifts in emotions often put children in situations that are misunderstood both by themselves and others. In many cases, children are unable to explain these emotions. They are just as much an enigma to them as they sometimes are to others. Emotional reactions can often be devastating to children as they try to adjust to different experiences that are tough to handle. Early adolescence is a time to examine these emotions, place them in perspective, and develop strategies to deal with them.

A Case Study of Philip

Philip Hall Likes Me. I Reckon Maybe
by
Bette Greene

A rural setting in Arkansas sets the stage for a story about a boy named Philip Hall. Philip is an eleven year old. He is energetic, inquisitive, and very proud to be a male. He has his own identity and feels secure to be a male. Philip is perceived as the smartest boy in the class. The dilemma begins as Beth Lambert, an eleven-year-old girl, gets a crush on Philip.

Beth, in her efforts to get Philip's attention, begins to maneuver her actions to convince Philip to socialize. She is also suspicious that Philip may not be the smartest. As the story progresses, they become involved in a mystery--the mystery of her father's missing turkeys. Their job as a team is to solve the mystery. Yet, with this teamship, they continue to compete with each other. This is amplified when they both raise calves to show at the fair. Beth's calf wins. Philip experiences shame. He no longer is perceived as a winner.

For the first time, Philip witnesses an emotion he never felt before—that of the pain of losing. Beth, being bothered by his pain, invites him to be her partner in a square dancing contest. This event, she feels, will help him overcome these feelings since this puts them in a position in which they will both either win or lose.

When Philip realizes what Beth had done, he admits that he did like her sometimes. Beth's dream comes true. Philip did not know how to handle the emotions that surfacde as he experienced failure for the first time. Through his interactions with his friend, Beth, these emotions become tolerable.

1. Is it ever difficult to be fair? What does being "fair" mean?

2. When you feel something is unfair, how do you react? Is this an appropriate reaction? How would you like to react differently next time?

3. What are some dilemmas or conflicts which you felt were unfair? How did these affect you?

4. When people disagree, how do you feel one should decide what to do in order to be fair to everyone involved?

5. What are some actions that would prevent someone from being unfair?

6. Who should decide what is fair and what is unfair? Why?

7. What happens that usually causes you to become angry, sad, or happy?

8. Describe a situation in which you and someone else reacted to the same situation in different ways. How do you explain this?

9. Describe an event in which you reacted in a way that you wished you had reacted differently. How do you wish you had reacted?

10. Have you ever had a feeling that you couldn't explain? How did you feel?

Related Early Adolescent Literature for
Additional Case Studies

Lois Lowry: *Anastasia Krupnik*

Valerie Flourney: *The Patchwork Quilt*

Bette Greene: *Philip Hall Likes Me. I Reckon Maybe*

Doris Buchanan Smith: *A Taste of Blackberries*

Judy Blume: *Tiger Eyes*

EXPLORATIONS

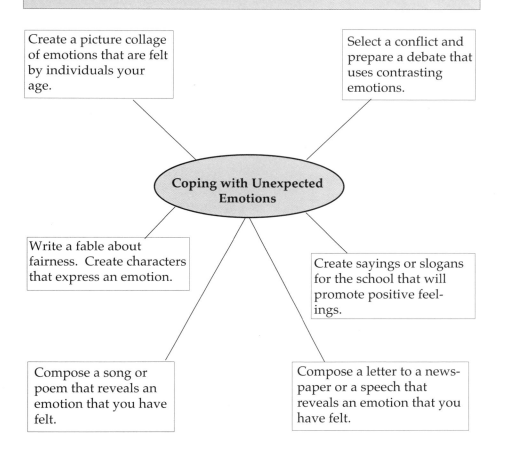

Create a picture collage of emotions that are felt by individuals your age.

Select a conflict and prepare a debate that uses contrasting emotions.

Coping with Unexpected Emotions

Write a fable about fairness. Create characters that express an emotion.

Create sayings or slogans for the school that will promote positive feelings.

Compose a song or poem that reveals an emotion that you have felt.

Compose a letter to a newspaper or a speech that reveals an emotion that you have felt.

PROBLEM SOLVING
Create a situation in which someone considers the action to be unfair: a grade, a punishment, election, sports events. Reveal in the story a reaction that could have been prevented had better communication among people existed.

Unit 7
Understanding the World

The considerable curiosity of youth is a feature that needs to be encouraged and nurtured.

The middle school years bring new curiosities among young adolescents. These curiosities are often grounded in their desire to know and their desire to make sense out of what they are experiencing and learning. These new intellectual capabilities need nurturing. Children often begin to question the validity of what they are learning. They often see very little application to their own lives. With the world becoming more complex, understanding the world may become even more complex. Too often, these new intellectual capabilities are not challenged or encouraged. In many cases, there is an assumption that children can handle abstract thought and make connections among the concepts and experiences they face. We forget that their physical size and age do not automatically reflect an ability to handle abstract thought.

The need to make connections among their experiences, to make connections among the skills that are developed and refined, and to understand the interdisciplinary nature of the world have been encouraged, yet little attention has been placed on helping our youth develop these skills. Children become concerned about health, behaviors, world issues and local problems; yet they are not yet equipped to conceptualize these without some guidance. Their need to understand the complexities of the world will lead to skills in making decisions, making contributions, and understanding how the world operates. As we all know, we use what we know in a way that makes sense to us. If we want youth to become active learners, have realistic understandings, develop lifelong skills, and make contributions, then we must provide opportunities for them to deepen these understandings. By engaging middle school children in examining authentic issues, they will begin to become decision-makers, apply their knowledge and skills, and understand the world.

A Case Study of James

How Many Miles To Babylon?
by
Paula Fox

The story of James is a story of a young ten year old who begins to discover himself, relationships, and the harshness of life. The experience faced by James is an experience of discovering one's heritage. He dreams of African royalty. In his attempt to establish an identity and discover that the world is a reasonable place, he thinks he was probably a prince whose ancestors had been marched across the land to boats that took them to slavery in a new country. His dreams include a story of his mother who travels to Africa to plan for his celebrated return. He goes to the basement of a dilapidated house to dress and dance like the African princes in photographs he had seen.

He soon encounters one of the harsh realities of the world. His friend wants him to help in stealing a valuable dog to earn reward money. They proceed to the amusement park. There his eyes are drawn to the Atlantic Ocean, which he had never seen. For the first time, he realized that the dream he had was only a dream—that his mother could not have crossed such a huge body of water.

His realization of the world and the realities that exist begins to separate his thoughts and pushes him into a situation in which he learns about life. His thoughts are not on himself. He plots to take the dogs with him, when he escapes, to return them to their owners. His return home illustrates the changed character who attempted to live in a dream—a dream that did not take into account reality. He learns that he is a strong person and that he does not have to rely on dreams and fantasy to solve his problems. He learns that he can be proud of who he is and that caring about others is important.

The story brings to the surface a story about a boy who widens his lens to the world, from a boyish look at life to one of an adult who looks at reality in a different way.

1. What are some topics or subjects you would like to know more about?

2. What are the most important topics or skills that individuals your age should be learning? Why?

3. What have you learned recently that caused you to think differently or that changed you?

4. When you had to learn something that you felt you did not need to know or want to know, how did you react? Why? What are some things you are asked to learn that you think are not important?

5. Have you ever learned something in one class that helped you in another class? How did it help?

6. What have you learned in school recently that you have used outside of school? Explain.

7. What was particularly difficult for you to learn? How did you deal with that?

8. Have you ever learned anything from a friend or family member that you feel was just as important as something you learned in school? What did you learn? From whom?

9. As you have gotten older, is learning more pleasant or less pleasant? In what way? Why?

10. What strategies do you feel make it easier for you to learn new things? Give an example.

Related Early Adolescent Literature for Additional Case Studies

Frances Goodrich and Albert Hackett: *The Diary of Anne Frank*

Gary Paulsen: *Woodsong*

Scott O'Dell: *Zia*

Jean Craighead George: *Julie of the Wolves*

Brenda Seabrooke: *Home is Where They Take You In*

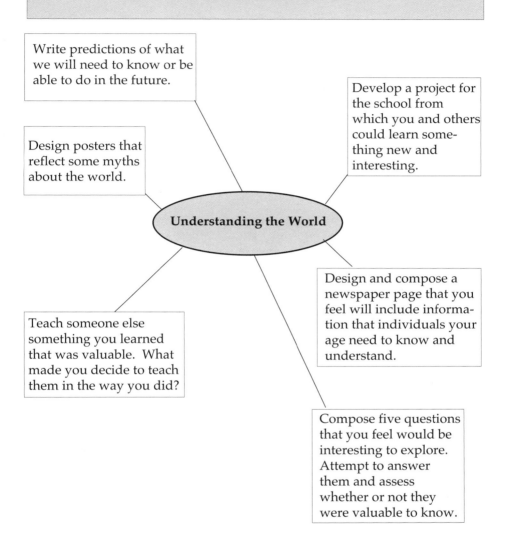

EXPLORATIONS

Write predictions of what we will need to know or be able to do in the future.

Develop a project for the school from which you and others could learn something new and interesting.

Design posters that reflect some myths about the world.

Understanding the World

Teach someone else something you learned that was valuable. What made you decide to teach them in the way you did?

Design and compose a newspaper page that you feel will include information that individuals your age need to know and understand.

Compose five questions that you feel would be interesting to explore. Attempt to answer them and assess whether or not they were valuable to know.

PROBLEM SOLVING

Select a mystery of the world. Why is it a mystery? Why is it a mystery worth exploring? How will solving the mystery benefit you?

Unit 8
Dealing With Difficult Questions

No question that occupies the minds of young adolescents should be viewed as too difficult to examine.

Interactions with early adolescents soon uncover those profound questions that occupy the minds of many young people. These questions, however, are often difficult to answer in a way that makes sense. Many of the questions young adolescents ask either deal with personal concerns that are confusing or abstract and do not have simple, concrete answers. They need assistance in coping with the inevitable day-to-day decisions these questions pose in their lives outside of school. Too often, however, young adolescents fear asking those questions lest they appear out of control or that they would be revealing thoughts that may be viewed by others as inappropriate. Often young adolescents have questions that may be perceived as flaws in their personality.

Young adolescents have strong concerns about physical, social, and moral issues. They witness others coping in ways that they do not understand. In many cases, they feel that they are alone in their desire to seek answers to these questions; therefore, many of our young people think silently, ponder, and attempt to answer the questions themselves. With this often comes misconceptions, confusion, and feelings of inadequacy. By providing opportunities for children to feel secure and safe in posing these difficult questions, children begin to understand that questions are in many ways natural parts of growing up. In fact, many of the questions children ask as the world becomes more complex are questions that adults have not yet answered. Children need to feel that the way we learn and grow is partially fulfilled through the use of inquiry—to seek answers that will provide the tools for making decisions.

A Case Study of Margaret

Are You There God? It's Me, Margaret.
by
Judy Blume

Margaret Simon is an only child who privately talks to God. She keeps her conversations with God a secret because if her parents know about these "talks," they'd think she "was some kind of religious fanatic or something." In fact, she can talk "to Him without moving her lips if she has to."

Margaret has concerns which are typical of twelve year olds. She worries about being flat-chested, not growing, and not wearing a bra. She is growing her hair and hopes that it will be "bouncy" like her friend Nancy's. She and her friends wonder how it feels to get their period. She asks God whether she should belong to the Y or the Jewish Community Center.

Margaret and her family's move to New Jersey seems to have made religion "the big thing in her life." She had lived in New York eleven and a half years and nobody had ever asked about her religion. Now everyone—friends and teachers—began asking questions. Margaret's mother was a Christian; her father, Jewish. Her mother's parents, who lived in Ohio, didn't want a Jewish son-in-law. Her father's family, Grandma Sylvia, "wasn't happy about getting a Christian daughter-in-law, but she at least accepted the situation." Because of the family conflict, her parents eloped and Margaret didn't "belong to any religion." Her parents hoped that Margaret would choose her "own" when she grew up. Margaret hated religious holidays. One of her dilemmas is choosing a religion. When assigned an individual project for her sixth grade class, Margaret decided to "know all there is to know about religion," since she has "never been inside a temple or a church." Then she'll "be able to join the Y or the Center like everybody else."

Her first religious experience was to attend temple services for Rosh Hosanna (New Year). The service was conducted in English and in Hebrew. Although Margaret tried hard to understand the Rabbi's sermon she gave up and started counting hats in the first five rows—eight brown, six black, three red, a yellow, and a leopard!

Margaret's second religious experience was attending the First Presbyterian Church with her friend, Janie. Margaret describes the church service as being "just like a temple except it was all in English." They "read from a prayer book that didn't make sense and the minister gave a sermon I couldn't follow."

Margaret's participation in the school's Christmas-Hanukkah pageant for parents creates confusion for her. Although the sixth-grade class was the choir, several children decided that singing either Christmas or Hanukkah songs was against their religion; therefore, they either marched and didn't sing or marched but "didn't even move their lips during the Hanukkah songs." She explains to God "I'm trying to decide if one (religion) might be special for me." "I haven't come up with any answers."

The social occasion of the year is a supper party at Norman (a drip) Fishbein's house. The whole class was invited. During the course of the evening, some members of the class engaged in "hanky-panky." Mrs. Fishbein was simply shocked by this "abominable behavior."

On Christmas Eve, Margaret attends services at the United Methodist Church with her friend, Nancy. She "enjoyed most of the service, especially since there wasn't any sermon." This experience confuses Margaret more than ever." "What religion should I be?" she asks God.

Margaret's Jewish Grandmother, Sylvia, loves her a lot. She takes Margaret to Lincoln Center in New York City, sends her a hundred-dollar savings bond every birthday plus new sweaters with MADE ESPECIALLY FOR YOU . . . BY GRANDMA labels in them. For spring vacation, Margaret is scheduled to visit Grandma in Florida—flying round trip all by herself. Then "Everything is wrong. Absolutely everything!" Unexpected company seems destined to cancel the long-awaited-for trip. Was God punishing her "for being a horrible person?" A confrontation between Margaret's mother's parents (absent from her life for fourteen years) and Margaret's parents anger Margaret. She decides "never to talk to God again."

The concerns and problems that Margaret faces are very real. In her last conversation, she confides "Are you still there, God. It's me, Margaret. I know you're there God. I know you wouldn't have missed this for anything! Thank you, God. Thanks an awful lot . ."

1. What questions have you asked your parents that helped you face some personal conflicts?

2. Do individuals your age feel comfortable asking adults personal questions? Why? What adults do you feel treat you seriously?

3. Have you ever had questions about growing up that were answered by your friends, then you discovered later that they were wrong? How can you prevent this?

4. Why do they think adults are sometimes unwilling to talk to you about your questions and problems?

5. What are some differences in growing up as a girl and growing up as a boy? Should there be differences?

6. Do you think you should be allowed to express the differences you have from adults? Why?

7. What do you feel young people value? Why?

8. How do you think you differ from your parents when they were your age?

9. Is it a good idea to allow people to decide what they share with others? Give an example.

10. What is the most important thing you have learned about yourself in the last year?

Related Early Adolescent Literature for Additional Case Studies

Judy Blume: *Then Again, Maybe I Won't*

Judy Blume: *Blubber*

Judy Blume: *Deenie*

Vera Cleaver: *Sweetly Sings the Donkey*

EXPLORATIONS

If you could talk to God like Margaret did, what concerns would you discuss with him/her? What actions would you ask God to take?

Develop a list of Margaret's personality traits. Cite specific examples from the story which make you think as you do. What attributes do you consider as positive personality traits? Negative? What makes you think as you do?

On the first day of sixth grade, Margaret wears her brown loafers without socks. Her mother thought it was dumb and advised against it. What good advice have your parents given but you refused to heed it?

Dealing with Difficult Questions

How would you grade Margaret's sixth grade project if you were Mr. Benedict?

Margaret wore loafers without socks because "Nancy says nobody in the sixth grade wears socks on the first day of school!" What advice have friends given you which turned out "painful" for you?

Margaret finds out that Nancy lied to her about her period. React to the statement, "What can you say when you've just found out your friend is a liar?"

PROBLEM SOLVING
A friend comes to you with a personal problem that is serious—contemplating drugs or suicide. What would you do to show you care, but at the same time, make decisions about how to seek help.

50

AREA II
Understanding Relationships

Those who understand early adolescents know very clearly the desire of young adolescents to socialize and feel accepted. During the early adolescent years, social groups become a central guide for the feelings, actions, and beliefs of ten to fourteen year olds. Like most new experiences, socialization is a complex process. Understanding relationships and the dynamics of forming relationships are best learned in situations in which individuals feel a need to belong and a need to understand interactions.

The struggle to form relationships evolves as children begin to break away from parents to establish their own identity, yet at the same time retaining those links they need from significant adults. Disappointments appear as young people discover that relationships change and that forming relationships is in itself a complex process that brings with it inconsistencies and diverse sets of rules and expectations. The need to be a part of a peer group, and at the same time retain and develop significant relationships with adults, often results in conflict. Values are being shaped and reshaped. Discoveries are being made about individuals and their own weaknesses and strengths. Elkind's *The Hurried Child* (1981) reflects many of these conflicts faced by young adolescents as they enter a world that is imperfect. Yet young adolescents have not yet developed an understanding of this imperfection. They soon discover that relationships are not formed easily and are not always predictable.

The changes in society faced by young people in the nineties have caused a wider range of roles to play in order to develop healthy relationships. Young people now face challenges not faced by early adolescents. They are often placed in situations which they are ill equipped to handle: divorce, drugs, teenage pregnancy, and others. No longer can children rely on relationships among adults to be carefree and easy to describe. Social changes have resulted in a new complex world of relationships.

Current early adolescent literature brings to readers characters who encounter these conflicts as they strive to develop relationships. These diverse conflicts provide opportunities for involving early adolescents in reflecting on their own struggles with relationships.

Unit 9
Desire for Peer Acceptance

Socialization and the development of relationships with one's peers create a sense of belonging.

The richness of the early adolescent years lies in the social interactions that form the basis for many of the behaviors that surface. Relationships offer a context in which children can test ideas, experiment with language, shape their identity, and form their own value system. Interpersonal relationships, then, occupy a major role in the lives of early adolescents. The fluidity of these relationships often brings frustrations and disappointments. Early adolescents experience traumatic conflicts due to conflicting loyalties to peer groups and family. Positive relationships can best be achieved in situations that provide ample opportunities for interactions. Relationships have their ups and downs during the early adolescent years. The need to experience positive relationships among their peer groups and with meaningful adults is critical to the development of positive attitudes about self and others. Adult values and loyalties are shaped conceptually during these early adolescent years. Negative interactions have a lasting impression on young people. In order to be accepted by others and to establish a sense of belonging, healthy humane attitudes are vital concerns during the early adolescent years.

A Case Study of Jeffrey

Maniac Magee
by
Jerry Spinelli

Maniac Magee is a modern tall tale. Jeffrey Lionel Magee, also known as "Maniac," is probably called that name because of his outrageous life-style. He doesn't attend school and lives in a variety of unusual environments, including the zoo. The history of Maniac is described as "one part fact, two parts legend, and three parts snowball." He can run like the wind, untie sneaker knots quicker that a kid could spend a quarter, and seems unaware of the traditions of racial segregation in the small Pennsylvania town of Two Mills.

Maniac became an orphan at the age of three. His parents had left him with a sitter and had taken the P & W high speed trolley into the city. On the way back home, the P & W had its famous crash. "The motor man was drunk and took the high trestle over the Schuylkill River at sixty miles an hour, and the whole kadoodle took a swan dive in the water. And just like that Maniac was an orphan."

After his parents' death, Maniac is sent off to his nearest relatives, Aunt Don and Uncle Dan. Living with two people who hated each other for eight years proved very difficult. After the Spring Musical, Maniac started running. "Never again to return to the house of two toasters. Never again to return to school."

Maniac begins his search for a home. His search for a home touches the lives of many people in the town of Two Mills, Pennsylvania. Maniac's first home was with the warm, loving Beales of the East End. From the Beales he learns what a loving family can mean. However, Maniac soon realizes that a white boy living in a black family's home could cause the family too much trouble. The buffalo pen at the zoo became Maniac's home until he is discovered by Earl Grayson, a park maintenance man. Grayson was once a professional baseball pitcher in the Appalachian League, Class D. Maniac teaches Grayson to read while Grayson teaches Maniac about baseball. Grayson dies soon after Christmas, and Maniac begins to drift again. This time he finds himself with the men-only McNabs, a white family who lives in the West End. Maniac has seen some amazing things in his lifetime, but nothing as amazing as that house. A total disaster! Cans and bottles lay all over, along with crusts, peelings, cores, scraps, rinds, wrappers—everything you would normally find in a garbage can. The McNabs are so fearful of the blacks of the East Side that they fortify their house in preparation for the revolt. "Let the rebels come. Let 'em bust through the newly installed bars over the plywood on the windows. Let 'em bust through the steel door. They'll find themselves staring down the barrel of a little surprise." They squabble over what the surprise would be. Uzi. AK-47. Bazooka. The coup de grace occurred when the Maniac brings a black friend, Mars Bar Thomson, to a birthday party at the McNabs. Subsequent occurrences help begin to break down long-lasting barriers between blacks and whites in Two Mills, Pennsylvania.

Adapted from *Language Arts*
January, 1993

QUESTIONS FOR DISCUSSION AND JOURNAL WRITING

1. Is it important to respect and value differences among people? What differences do you value?

2. In what ways do you think you can get to know other people?

3. How do you determine whether or not to initiate a relationship with another person? What qualities do you look for?

4. Has there been a situation in which your friends have not accepted others because of the way they talked, dressed, or looked? What problem do you see in this? How could this be changed?

5. Is it possible to be yourself and still be accepted by others who are different from you? How do you think you can accomplish this?

6. Describe five difficult actions that are needed to develop positive relationships with others. How do you deal with these?

7. Why do relationships with your friends change?

8. What do you do when you feel you are excluded from a group in which you want to be a part?

9. For individuals your age, what are the reasons friendships are important?

10. Can you be friends with adults? Why? How?

Related Early Adolescent Literature for
Additional Case Studies

Julia Cunningham: *Burnish Me Bright*

Susan Pfeiffer: *What Do You Do When Your Mouth Won't Open?*

Bette Greene: *Philip Hall Likes Me. I Reckon Maybe.*

Jean Little: *Take Wing*

Paula Danzinger: *The Pistachio Prescription*

Develop a character web of words to describe Maniac Magee. Include a reason for each description you have chosen.

Compose a biographical sketch of individuals with whom you have developed a positive relationship.

Interview three or four individuals and describe what you have in common, what you learned from the individuals, and/or qualities you find interesting about the people.

Desire for Peer Acceptance

Maniac is allergic to pizza. Write a paragraph describing allergies you may have and how your body reacts? Write a paragraph explaining what you would like to have as an allergy and explain why you have chosen this particular allergy.

Chapter 27 describes how Grayson learns to read. How do you define "reading." Explain the definition of reading. How would you go about teaching someone to read?

Design an imaginary person with whom you would like to be a friend.

If you could chose an "ideal" place to live, where would you live and why would you choose to live there.

PROBLEM SOLVING

Sometimes we have misunderstandings among our friends or family. Describe one of these misunderstandings and then make recommendations about how you could regain that relationship after a disagreement or misunderstanding.

Unit 10
Adjusting To a New Situation

Experience with new situations must be grounded in the desire to know and supported with a sense of trust and respect.

Facing the unknown and mysterious may be uncomfortable for some adolescents. The changes are so overwhelming for young adolescents that adjusting to a new situation seems to compound the confusion and questions they face. The search for consistency in a time when there is very little consistency is a major concern for many young adolescents. The feeling of inadequacy and the fear of being discovered as one who is not in control makes adjusting to a new situation something to fear. The fear of failure and the recognition of inadequacies in how to handle new powers of intellectual and social interactions make new situations very threatening events. Therefore, a tendency to avoid the situation or resist new encounters develops.

Expectations begin to change. Young adolescents face changing adult and peer expectations. Often, they have to take on adult responsibilities that they are not equipped to handle. They begin to fear they will face rejection unless they are successful in their experimentations with new skills and thoughts. The need to assist young adolescents in adjusting to a new situation brings new confidence, trust, and a sense of control. Young adolescents must come to realize that making mistakes, and facing changes are safe and should be encouraged. Strategies to assist young adolescents in adjusting to these new situations offer them opportunities to experiment socially, intellectually, and physically in safe, caring environments that support change, not discourage it.

A Case Study of Mary

Where The Lilies Bloom
by
Vera and Bill Cleaver

The problem of a family's struggle to cope without the benefit of two parents is presented in the story of Mary Call. Mary is fourteen. She is presented with a situation requiring a decision. Her conflict is her desire to keep a promise she made to her dying father and her realization that she must break that promise in order to ensure her family's survival. Often, children are placed in a predicament in which they are faced with new challenges—often adult challenges. Such a challenge may lead to a strengthening of character, yet Mary is only fourteen and still a developing child.

The story of a girl who faces a conflict between how she was raised and the realities of life surface when she remembers that her father was one who lived by a strong family moral code—protect the family, instill family pride, teach that pride to others who follow, carry on the family traditions. Mary, however, realizes that she is young and that she may not be able to carry out her father's wishes by herself.

Growing up, she respected her father and believed the story she was told about the ill feelings he had about the oldest daughter and the despised neighbor, Kaiser Pease. Through time, she realized that the stories were not true and that her father had made a mistake.

Faced with the realization that her father was wrong, Mary begins to experience a new situation—one that places her in a position of making choices that she is ill equipped to handle and, at the same time, struggles between the strong moral code that her father established and the realization that he had weaknesses. Such a discovery places Mary in a situation that might have been beyond her capabilities. From this situation, however, Mary learns a valuable lesson about life—that adults do make errors and that decisions have to be made after the truth is known.

1. What is most difficult about change for you? Who do you go to for help when you are faced with changes that confuse you?

2. What are you able to do better with the help of others? What are you able to do better by yourself?

3. How do you think it would feel to be isolated from people you know and respect?

4. Describe some people, activities, items that would be difficult for you to do without. How would you deal with these changes?

5. Is it always important to approach a new situation by yourself? When? When do you feel you would need help or guidance?

6. What new tasks or situations have you encountered that were not pleasant? How do you deal with these?

7. What is a situation that you feared, but after you got involved, it wasn't as difficult as you expected?

8. What are you expected to do that you feel you have received adequate help or preparation to do?

9. Do you feel you can accomplish any new situation if you have the desire? Explain and give an example.

10. Are there situations you feel you were prepared to do, but once you got involved, it wasn't as easy as you thought? Describe one.

Related Early Adolescent Literature for Additional Case Studies

Judy Blume: *Are You There God? It's Me , Margaret.*

Betsy Byars: *The Animal, Vegetable and John D. Jones*

Gary Paulsen: *Hatchet*

Jean Fritz: *The Cabin Faced West*

Barthe DeClements: *Nothing's Fair In Fifth Grade*

Compose a time line of new situations you want to experience. How will you prepare yourself for these?

Teach someone or assist someone in dealing with a new situation.

Go without a needed item for a day: a pencil, a shoe, a comb, etc. At the end, describe how you felt. How did you adjust?

Adjusting To A New Situation

Compose one page of hints to help a new person become oriented to your school, solve a problem, or perform a task.

Make a list of new situations you encountered over the last year. What did you do to help? What were the results? How would you have made them easier?

Collect photographs of new experiences that you encountered—vacation to the beach, birthday, etc. What do you remember about these?

PROBLEM SOLVING
Create a set of school rules that would alienate people or prevent people from having personal freedoms. Explain how you feel people would feel and how they could adjust.

Unit 11
Developing Family Relationships

Family relationships provide the security and guidance early adolescents need to become productive, secure individuals.

Despite what many may say about young adolescents, studies indicate that early adolescence is a time in which there is a strong desire for significant adults in their lives, including family. The need for belonging is apparent as they seek frequent affirmation of their worth and place in the world. Feelings of adult rejection may be present. Vast changes in the family structure have resulted in many children being left to guide themselves, to search for other significant adults. Carnegie's *Turning Points: Preparing American Youth for the 21st Century* (1989) outlines some of the many social and family-oriented changes that have occurred and the need to provide additional support for children during the early adolescent years. As children grow and begin to cope with their rapid changes, a strong sense of belonging becomes more important. The security they need is often shattered in their lives as homes become fragmented. Many children find themselves cast into situations for which they are not prepared such as increased responsibilities when a parent dies or moves away. Self-blame often occurs in divorce situations. Children who have a sense of belonging and who have a well-developed sense of what family means tend to have more opportunities for developing the security they need to make decisions about their own lives.

A Case Study of Lily

Sweetly Sings the Donkey
by
Vera Cleaver

Lily Snow, like other contemporary teenagers, is a tangle of complex and warring emotions and dreams. At times she is the quintessential emerging woman, aware of men and boys being drawn to her. She can also be universal earth mother to her family. Yet she may just as quickly turn tomboy or petulant child.

As a member of a dysfunctional family, in which the children often are more adult than their parents, Lily as the oldest and strongest becomes and accepts the role of family matriarch. Before her weak mother's final desertion, she makes Lily promise not to leave the family when they go to Florida. In the end, it is this 14-year-old's strength of will and boundless energy that holds the family together.

Childlike in her hope that the move to Florida will let them "leave their aches behind," she does not allow the reality of their new life to daunt her. Though she shares the dreaminess of her ineffectual father, there is a basic difference. Lily is willing to plan, work, and enlist the help of others in making her dreams for a real family home come true. She is a fighter willing to use her brain, her physical strength, and yes —her feminine wiles. She is a modern pioneer woman.

Though there is sadness in seeing one so young accept adult responsibilities as so many adolescents must, the vibrancy of Lily's personality and her exuberant bursts of energy and hope paint a positive picture. She is not a drab, despondent survivor. Rather, she is a victorious warrior. She becomes a whole person able to accept the reality she finds, but not the kind of person to passively accept. She realizes she can shape her future and does so.

Questions for Discussion and Journal Writing

1. What does it mean to be a "family?" In what ways have you experienced this?

2. What are three things you wish your family would do to show it understands you better?

3. What are some actions you could take as a family member that would establish a stronger family relationship?

4. What are some memorable moments in your family? What are some moments which you wish had not occurred?

5. What changes have taken place in your family that caused some confusion, disagreements or conflicts? How were these solved?

6. What family member(s) can you go to when you need something? Why or why not? How could you assist in changing this relationship or strengthening this relationship?

7. Are there adults, other than your family, you feel you can go to when you need help? Who? Why?

8. What are some family situations that you have observed that are admirable?

9. Are there family expectations you know exist that you feel are beyond your capabilities?

10. How does your family show you that you are valuable?

Related Early Adolescent Literature for
Additional Case Studies

Wilson Rawls: *Where the Red Fern Grows*

Sue Ellen Bridgers: *Home Before Dark*

Patricia MacLachlan: *Sarah, Plain and Tall*

Beverly Cleary: *Ramona and Her Father*

Paula Danzinger: *Can You Sue Your Parents for Malpractice?*

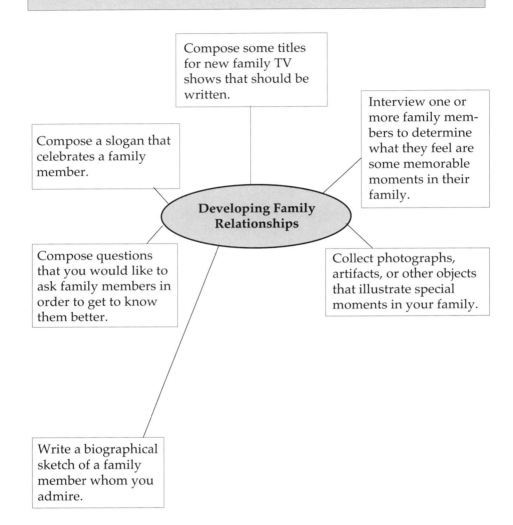

Compose some titles for new family TV shows that should be written.

Interview one or more family members to determine what they feel are some memorable moments in their family.

Compose a slogan that celebrates a family member.

Developing Family Relationships

Compose questions that you would like to ask family members in order to get to know them better.

Collect photographs, artifacts, or other objects that illustrate special moments in your family.

Write a biographical sketch of a family member whom you admire.

PROBLEM SOLVING
Find out about your ancestors—where they lived, what they did for a living—and construct a family tree.

Unit 12
Understanding and Appreciating Diverse Cultures

While all people may not share the same personal beliefs and values, they all share basic human needs.

The mobility of people in the United States have made it important for children to become aware of differences among people from varied cultures. Different cultural backgrounds bring more diverse life-styles that add to the questions and inconsistencies that early adolescents face. The understanding and appreciation of such differences become important as children develop their own sense of self and the world. In many cases, their view of the world is limited to their own existence. Yet, as the world becomes more complex, they encounter even more diversity. Myths about people from other cultures exist that lead to more confusion in their lives. Diversity can be viewed as good or bad. What children must experience are the positive aspects of diversity, while recognizing the problems that occur with diversity. Such views are often hard for early adolescents to conceptualize, especially if they experience conflicting views in their own lives from people around them. Experiences that encourage young adolescents to value the richness of diversity will help them realize that diversity makes us stronger and more able to act in caring ways toward people.

A Case Study of Elizabeth

Zeely
by
Virginia Hamilton

Elizabeth, soon after going to her Uncle Ross's farm, begins to discover some profound things about people. Elizabeth is an inquisitive individual, adventurous, and a risk-taker. She calls herself "Geeder" and even renames her brother. Her imagination is heightened when the story begins to bring her together with a neighbor, Miss Zeely Tayber.

Elizabeth's first impression of Miss Zeely is one that changes her life. Miss Zeely is a tall, stately black lady. From pictures of Watusi queens, Elizabeth comes to believe that Miss Zeely looks like the queen and probably is. Like many young adolescents, she begins to tell her friends about the Watusi queen. As the story progresses and as she interacts with Miss Zeely, she comes to realize that being a queen like the ones in books with servants and great castles, is not what being a human being is about. This is not what makes a great person—a queen as she says. What people feel is what makes greatness.

In a time in which children form their views of others by what they hear and read, many myths evolve. In an attempt to become important, Elizabeth realizes a new level of importance to her heritage. People are different culturally, but are the same in their emotions of fear, love, and compassion. Elizabeth realizes this as she gets to know people, as she begins to form new images of her life and her heritage. Her search for her roots in the African past illustrates her concern about her heritage.

1. What is special about understanding individuals from another culture?

2. Do you think there are some commonalities among all people? What are some? What are some of the differences? Why do they exist?

3. What is it about your culture that you respect and desire? How would you feel if these features were different?

4. What are some questions you have about people from different cultures?

5. What are the best ways to get to know people from other cultures?

6. How could you help people from other cultures adjust to the culture in which you live?

7. Is there a "better culture?" Why?

8. What are some of your reflections on your own culture?

9. Do you feel you would be a better person if you had contact with people from other cultures? How can exposure to another culture help you?

10. Describe what you feel it would be like to be accepted by only those who are like you?

Related Early Adolescent Literature for
Additional Case Studies

Lawrence Yep: *Dragonwings*

Scott O'Dell: *Island of the Blue Dolphins*

Robert Burch: *Queenie Peavy*

Gary Paulsen: *Dogsong*

Elizabeth Speare: *Sign of the Beaver*

EXPLORATIONS

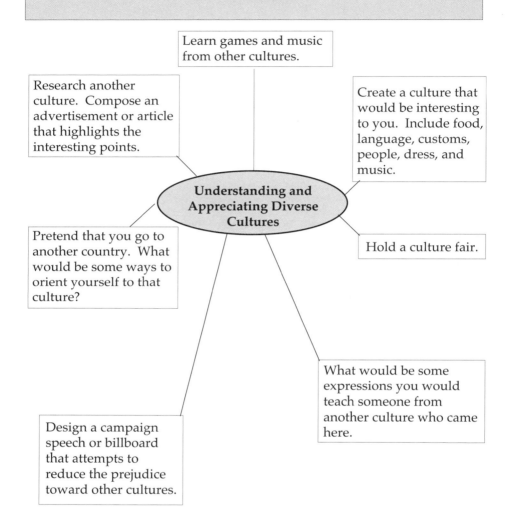

Learn games and music from other cultures.

Research another culture. Compose an advertisement or article that highlights the interesting points.

Create a culture that would be interesting to you. Include food, language, customs, people, dress, and music.

Understanding and Appreciating Diverse Cultures

Pretend that you go to another country. What would be some ways to orient yourself to that culture?

Hold a culture fair.

Design a campaign speech or billboard that attempts to reduce the prejudice toward other cultures.

What would be some expressions you would teach someone from another culture who came here.

PROBLEM SOLVING
Pretend you are introduced to a teenager from another country who speaks very little English. How would you assist the student in becoming a part of your social group? If members of the group did not want to include the person, how could you deal with this?

Unit 13
Coping With Divorce

The actuality of divorce often places young adolescents in a struggle to keep the family together.

The increase in the number of young people who experience one or more changes in their family structure during their preadolescent years has created new dilemmas for our youth. New questions, new decisions, new conflicts have made it difficult for them to grow into healthy, productive individuals. Faced with the possibility of a single parent family, or perhaps living in a foster home or with grandparents, many young adolescents face new challenges. Not only is it difficult to be a young adolescent, it is more traumatic if extra worries are added. Children often are taught to respect family, to love and respect others, yet they experience adults around them who do not demonstrate these practices. Their questions become obvious ones. Why did they do this? What will I do now? Who will I go to for help? Who will I live with?

Middle school children search and find value in a significant adult. Many times, these are parents. Yet, divorce often reduces that security. Children often blame themselves. Torn between coping with their own individual problems and concerns, they now have to contend with adult problems. Often, they are asked to take on new responsibilities for which they are not equipped: taking care of a grandparent or a sibling, for example. They see these actions as interferences. Children need to have opportunities to express their questions and concerns, to know that they are secure and safe, and to feel that they will be fine. They need to understand what is happening to adults—why divorce occurs. Many of these individuals are at a time in which pressures to act out adult roles are encouraged: sex, early marriage, commitment to one individual from the opposite sex. They see inconsistencies within the lives of the adults that contrast with what they were told to believe: compassion for others, loyalty, trust. In many cases they are told that arguments do not solve problems, yet they see arguments. They are told not to abuse an individual, yet they often see physical and verbal abuse. The realities of divorce bring a new dimension of development for children.

A Case Study of Leigh

Dear Mr. Henshaw
by
Beverly Cleary

Leigh Marcus Botts is an only child who is trying to adjust to his parents' divorce. The story is told through Leigh's letters to his favorite author and through his diary entries. Leigh learns to use his writing as a vehicle for expressing his feelings and for thinking through his problems. He comes to accept the changes that have taken place in his life.

Leigh was introduced to Mr. Boyd Henshaw when his second grade teacher read his book, *Ways to Amuse a Dog*. Leigh describes the book as "the first thick book with chapters I read in the third grade." In the fourth grade, Leigh makes a diorama for the book. When his teacher makes the students write to authors for Book Week, Leigh writes to Mr. Henshaw for the third time. Offended by having received a letter from Mr. Henshaw that was "only printed," he encourages Mr. Henshaw to "write to me in your own handwriting" because Leigh describes himself as "a great enjoyer of your books."

Leigh's great love of dogs is revealed in a variety of ways. He describes his favorite character in the book, *Ways to Amuse a Dog*, as Joe's father because Joe's father didn't get mad when Joe amused the dog by playing a tape of a lady singing, to which his dog howled along. Later Leigh reveals his disgust with mobile home park living because "mostly real old grown-ups with cats get mad if dogs aren't on leashes every minute." It's not surprising that the sequel to *Dear Mr. Henshaw*, *Strider*, is a continuing story of the life of Leigh Botts and his new dog. It becomes apparent that Leigh is impressed with the responses of Mr. Henshaw when again in sixth grade "in a new school in a different town" he writes to the author in order to fulfill his teacher's assignment designed "to improve our writing skills." Although Leigh has no difficulty asking Mr. Henshaw ten lengthy questions and demanding "a list of your books that you write, an autographed picture and a bookmark," he stubbornly refuses to answer ten questions asked by Mr. Henshaw until his mother discovers the questions "lying around." Leigh reluctantly answers the questions over a period of time mostly because the TV is broken or he is bored.

Over the span of five years you find out that:

- Leigh is a plain, not stupid, "mediumest" boy in the class

- Since the divorce Leigh lives with his Mom in a really little house in Pacific Grove. Dad got the custody of the dog, Bandit. The house is located next to a gas station.

- Mom works part-time for Catering by Katie and takes courses at a Community College to be an LVN (Licensed Vocational Nurse).

- The circumstances under which Bandit came to live with Leigh's family and how Bandit got his name.

- Leigh recently moved to a new school, doesn't have many friends, and as a result, is lonesome. The cautious side of his personality is revealed when he says "A new boy in school has to be pretty cautious until he gets to know who's who."

- His favorite teacher is the custodian, Mr. Fridley. Mr. Fridley is described as fair, doesn't get cross even when somebody "whoops it up." He is sort of "baggy" and comfortable like a grandfather.

- Leigh is bothered by someone stealing morsels out of his lunch bag, little kids with runny noses, having to walk "slow" to school, and his Dad's constant remark when and if he calls, "Well, keep your nose clean kid."

- Leigh longs for a closer relationship with his father who is a cross-country truck driver and who sometimes forgets to call or "to send this month's support payment." Leigh finally learns "by now that I couldn't count on anything he said."

- Leigh feels better when he writes in his diary and his writing skills improve. After a while he doesn't even have to pretend to write to Mr. Henshaw.

- Burglar-proofing his lunch box by making a burglar alarm makes Leigh realize that people at school, including the principal, did notice him and that other people had experienced things stolen items from their lunches. This notoriety makes Leigh feel "like some sort of hero." Maybe "not so medium after all."

- Doing things like reading, writing, and scrubbing off the mildew in the bathroom are easier to do if the reason for doing them is relevant. Finally he also realizes that he needs to write honestly about something he knows and has strong feelings about.

1. What do you think are some reasons adults get divorced? Are there any justifiable reasons? What are they?

2. What problems are created for children when parents divorce? What do you think parents should do to help the situation, especially for the children?

3. What can children do to adjust to a family that has just gone through a divorce? Who can children talk to in order to share feelings, ask questions, and state concerns?

4. As a result of divorce, are there extra conflicts that adolescents face? What are these? How can they cope?

5. If you have a friend who just experienced a divorce in the family, what can you do to help him or her?

6. What kind of preparation is needed for you to get ready for the time in which you may be considering marriage? What information do you need to know?

7. Does divorce mean that parents stop loving their children? Why do children feel this way sometimes?

8. What do you feel would prepare you for the possibility of your parents' divorce?

9. What does "loyalty" mean? Is it difficult to be loyal to people you love? Why?

10. Who is an adult friend who could help you if you faced a divorce in your family? Why did you select this adult?

Related Early Adolescent Literature for
Additional Case Studies

Peggy Mann: *My Dad Lives in a Downtown Hotel*

Betsy Byars: *The Animal, Vegetable and John D. Jones*

Carol Benjamin: *The Wicked Stepdog*

Marion Bauer: *Foster Child*

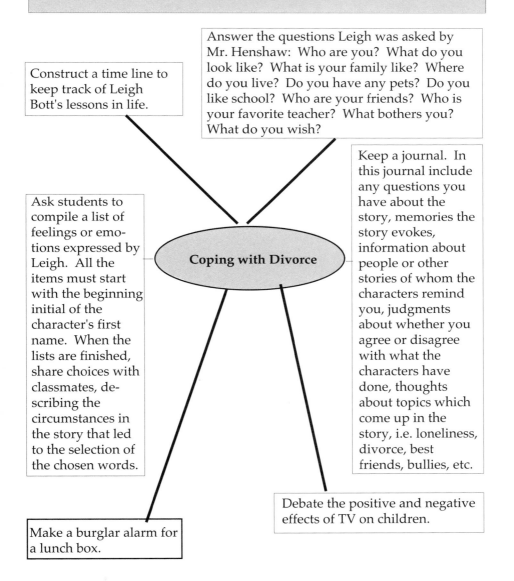

Construct a time line to keep track of Leigh Bott's lessons in life.

Answer the questions Leigh was asked by Mr. Henshaw: Who are you? What do you look like? What is your family like? Where do you live? Do you have any pets? Do you like school? Who are your friends? Who is your favorite teacher? What bothers you? What do you wish?

Keep a journal. In this journal include any questions you have about the story, memories the story evokes, information about people or other stories of whom the characters remind you, judgments about whether you agree or disagree with what the characters have done, thoughts about topics which come up in the story, i.e. loneliness, divorce, best friends, bullies, etc.

Ask students to compile a list of feelings or emotions expressed by Leigh. All the items must start with the beginning initial of the character's first name. When the lists are finished, share choices with classmates, describing the circumstances in the story that led to the selection of the chosen words.

Coping with Divorce

Debate the positive and negative effects of TV on children.

Make a burglar alarm for a lunch box.

PROBLEM SOLVING
Prepare a pamphlet for parents that will make suggestions about how to strengthen family relationships and encourage communication.

Unit 14
Dealing With Death

Even though facing death of a loved one is difficult, part of growing up is realizing and accepting the fact of death.

Unfortunately, death is a difficult experience for anyone to face. For children, the experience may be a new experience that brings additional doubts, uncertainties, and disorientation. The fear of losing a friend, a family member or a pet is compounded during the early adolescent years. Fear of death occupies many early adolescents' thoughts. What often comes with the death of a loved one or friend is an adjustment and new responsibilities that they are not yet equipped to handle. The loss of a parent, for example, may lead to having to take on new responsibilities. The death of a friend leads to a personal loss that leaves them feeling alone. Even though they may have an understanding intellectually of death, their ability to cope with the consequences are often devastating. What they see around them are variations in how individuals react to death. This reality becomes confusing in that they have not yet developed a strong understanding of human emotions. Their emotions are fluid. Helping young people deal with death becomes more critical today with the rise in teenage suicides, homicides, the AIDS epidemic, and other natural and unnatural causes of death among peers and family.

A Case Study of Trav, Buck, and Kate

Remembering the Good Times
by
Richard Peck

A friend's suicide is never an easy matter for a young adolescent. The story of Trav is one about a boy and his friends—Kate and Buck. Trav is angry and unsure of himself. He does not have a clear sense of direction and fears the future and what it might be. His parents are very successful, and Trav has the impression that he is expected to grow up and be like them.

The conflict begins when he begins to feel inadequate and fears the future. The struggles evolve when he questions the likelihood that he will grow up to be successful. More importantly, he fears that he will not develop the skills he needs to prepare for life. His relationships with his friends increase. Each is different. Kate is sure of herself. Buck, however, has no direction and wonders where he belongs. The threesome begin to interact, yet each offers the others very little help. Trav becomes more and more despondent. Expectations from his family increase the pressure and he takes his own life.

The reactions to the suicide vary. Kate, unable to understand what happened, admonishes herself and feels that she should have recognized the signs. School administrators blame the parents. The parents blame the school. Others blame the community.

The growth and realizations of facing death of a friend is witnessed as Kate and Buck begin to remember Trav and the good times they had. The story of Trav and his friends illustrates how friends are friends even in the time of tragedy and how thy rely on each other for comfort.

1. Describe an adult who understands you and with whom you feel you can talk if you have questions about death?

2. What are the central differences between how adults cope with death and how individuals your age cope with death?

3. When you think of the word "death" what comes to your mind? Why do you think these images surface?

4. What can you do if you suspect that a friend or family member may be in danger of death?

5. Identify an adult you feel comes closest to being able to support you if you were faced with the death of a friend or family member. Why did you select this person?

6. What are some questions you would like to ask about death or coping with death?

7. What are some signs that might warn you that possibly a friend may be considering suicide?

8. What do you need from others in order to help you cope with the death of a friend or family member?

9. Do you feel free to express your emotions when you are troubled? Explain. Give an example.

10. If a friend of yours died, what would help you not feel alone?

Related Early Adolescent Literature for Additional Case Studies

Doris Buchanan Smith: *A Taste of Blackberries*

Judy Blume: *Tiger Eyes*

Constance Greene: *Beat the Turtle Drum*

Peggy Mann: *There Are Two Kinds of Terrible*

Katherine Paterson: *Bridge to Terabithia*

Prepare a guide that would be useful in developing a positive attitude.

Compile a list of people to contact if you suspect someone is contemplating suicide.

In small groups, develop a list of suggestions that show how friends can support each other in coping with death.

Dealing with Death

Compose a poster to help others seek help if they face the death of a friend or family member.

Prepare a mural that illustrates families who support each other in a time of need.

Make a collage of an emotion related to death that you feel is natural.

PROBLEM SOLVING

Compose a story about a family who experiences the death of a family member. Include scenes that illustrate how the family adjusted to this loss.

Unit 15
Dealing With Aging

Becoming involved with the elderly offers opportunities to discover the human dignity, self-worth, and contributions of people of all ages.

Changes in the family structure have decreased the likelihood that young adolescents will have direct contact with the elderly in the home. The changing family structure prevents many young people from growing up in homes in which grandparents play a central role. As a result, many young people have little or no contact with the elderly, thus creating a void in their understanding of the aging process. Yet, because people now live longer, many of these young people will eventually come face to face with the realities of aging—parents reaching retirement, their own aging process, the work force with increased numbers of elderly people participating. Many young adolescents are not aware of those forces that affect the aging. How are they to grasp the realities of a complex world in which health plays a major role if they have little or no concept of aging? Opportunities to learn about aging should be provided in order to dispel the myths about aging. In many cases, our youth do not understand the unique problems and concerns that come with aging. Such preparation would not be too soon in the middle school years, for values are being shaped and understandings of people are being refined.

A Case Study of Peter

The War With Grandpa
by
Robert Kimmel Smith

Ten-year-old Peter is thrilled that Grandpa is coming to live with the Stokes family. That is, until Grandpa Jack moves right into Peter's wonderful room, forcing him to move to the dinky guest room on the third floor. He thinks the move is "disgusting, terrible, gross, and also horrible." While Peter loves his Grandpa, he also loves his room. It has always been his room all his life and he's fixed it just the way he likes it. "Nothing about my room is scary." Peter has no choice except to declare war on Grandpa in order to reclaim his stolen territory.

At first, Grandpa doesn't take Peter's declaration of war seriously. But Peter persists with such single-minded tenacity that Grandpa finally retaliates — and the war is on!

The War with Grandpa is full of prankish skirmishes and loving truces. Emotions on both sides range from anger to remorse. In the end, the relationship between Peter and Grandpa is preserved, and Peter realizes that war is not a solution to conflict, after all.

The story written as a fifth grade English assignment tells it "real and true." Peter is reminded to "put in words that people said, if we can remember, and to put quote marks around them and everything." He also admonishes himself to keep the sentences short using lots of chapters that are short. "This style of writing," according to Peter, "makes the book go faster and you always can find your place."

Grandpa is very depressed ever since Grandma's death. He is described by Peter as having "a sad look in his eyes even when he was smiling." "There is no life in him." All he does since moving back from Florida is sit around and mope all the time "except he calls it resting." When Peter declares war with a note typewritten on his father's typewriter, Grandpa fails to respond. Peter declares that Grandpa is "one of the world's greatest ignorers."

Steve Mayer and Billy Alston have been Peter's friends ever since kindergarten. Thinking that Peter is stupid "because you don't start a war with a note," they describe Grandpa as a "room robber" and encourage Peter to engage in "gorilla warfare" and "attack." They caution Peter to conceal his identity, however, "like Zorro or Batman and Robin."

Yielding to peer pressure Peter "attacks" by fixing the alarm to wake grandpa in the middle of the night. Grandpa tries to reason "Petey" out of the declaration of war. He describes his grandson as being "a little spoiled" because he's always had everything he's wanted — big house, lots of toys, good clothes, and plenty to eat. "You don't know about really wanting something and doing without."

In a second attempt at "gorilla warfare" Peter steals Grandpa's slippers. Unaware of Peter's determination, Grandpa tries again to dissuade Peter from "warfare." Peter's friends suggest that Grandpa doesn't want to fight and tries to retaliate by being "darn nice" so Peter will "forget the whole thing and call off the war." Feeling guilty about his actions against his Grandpa, Peter defends his Grandpa describing him as "just a good sweet man who loves me a lot." "So he forgave my stealing his slippers and lets me know by kissing me." Steve and Billy convince Peter that "the war is over . . . and you've lost."

Undaunted by two attacks, Grandpa, the determined pacifist, tries again to convince Peter about the uselessness of war. Frustrated with Peter's actions and continued lack of reason, he slaps Peter "hard across my cheek." His actions are designed to demonstrate to Peter that "war hurts, war wounds and kills and causes misery." "Only a fool wants war." This confrontation solidifies Peter's determination to regain his room.

Grandpa finally succumbs to the declaration of war. He takes Peter's Monopoly pieces as "prisoners of war" and advises Peter that "two can play at this game." Grandpa has seemed to get "his old pizzazz back."

Although Grandpa and Peter have a wonderful day fishing together — during which Peter learns to row a boat, clean fish and get the scales off — Peter attacks one more time. He steals Grandpa's wristwatch. The watch has great sentimental value to Grandpa having received it from Grandma as a gift for their 40th wedding anniversary. Grandpa finally understands. However, he admonishes "but from now on you'd better watch out."

Grandpa's revenge makes Peter realize that war is indeed hell! Peter's latest antics called for massive retaliation on Grandpa's part. The last attack by Peter consisted of a disgusting trick — stealing Grandpa's false teeth in the middle of the night—a terrible thing to do.

Seeing Grandpa without his teeth made him appear old and helpless. Peter's act made him declare the war's end. But the declaration of the war enabled Grandpa to get over his sadness. Peter lost the war by "the skin of Grandpa's teeth."

What did this writing assignment teach Peter? "Writing is mostly fun, but some of it is hard work." "If you wait long enough and think hard enough, and your sister keeps out of your hair, then you can do it." "Starting is the hardest part." "And it gets easier as you go along." And what will reading the book teach you about Peter and about the causes and effects of war?

1. How would you best describe people as they get older?

2. What questions do you and others your age have about the elderly?

3. What do elderly people and individuals your age have in common? How do you feel individuals your age could build relationships with those aging?

4. What do you feel you could learn from the elderly? What do you feel the elderly could learn from you?

5. Do you know an elderly person with whom you share the same qualities? What are they?

6. How can you contribute to the improvement of life for the elderly?

7. What would you like the elderly to know about individuals your age?

8. What are some fears you have of growing old?

9. What are the most significant current issues that pertain to the aging?

10. What have been some major contributions of the elderly?

Related Early Adolescent Literature for
Additional Case Studies

Natalie Babbitt: *Tuck Everlasting*

Gary Paulsen: *Tracker*

Tomie de Paola: *Nana Upstairs, Nana Downstairs*

Betsy Byars: *After the Goat Man*

Cynthia Voight: *Dicey's Song*

EXPLORATIONS

Pretend that you are responsible for taking care of an elderly person or spending some time with an elderly person. Describe a project that you could do with them.

Look at photographs of the elderly or TV characters. Describe what you see that may be misunderstood.

Describe what you think you will be like when you are older? Draw or write an autobiographical sketch of yourself.

Dealing with Aging

Brainstorm the characteristics of grandfathers. If possible, categorize these characteristics: physical traits, personalities, things grandfathers do, etc. Write a descriptive paragraph about your own grandpa or about an imaginary one.

In dialogue journals, react to the characters, how you would handle similar situations, compare what is happening in the book with real life situations, illustrate characters, setting, or actions.

Discuss alternatives to war. What might Peter have done with the same result (get his room back).

In small group discuss the way Mr. & Mrs. Stokes handled the decision of Grandpa moving into Peter's room. Decide if they handled their decision in the best possible way. Suggest alternative ways of handling this decision.

PROBLEM SOLVING

On a 5 x 8 card, have students write a paragraph concerning promises made to themselves beginning with "When I grow up and have a child, I will never make him or her . . ." In a second paragraph on the back of the card, ask students to write exceptions to the promise beginning with "However, I might make him or her … because …" Also list things they would make their children do and why.

Conclusion

This section of the monograph provided a plan for using current early adolescent literature as a vehicle for engaging young people in reflecting on their own development, their own questions, their own concerns, and their own experiences during adolescence. Part of the challenge is to encourage young adolescents to take the risk and talk among their peers. The excitement lies in the connections young adolescents make between their own dilemmas and the dilemmas faced by the book characters. The activities in the units are intended to involve young adolescents in active ways. However, they may change as the reflections and interactions move in different directions. The central goal is for students to engage in acts of genuine reflection—what they say, feel, and think. The utilization of these units needs to be examined, extended, and tailored to one's own situation. The next section examines some of those alternatives.

Constructing additional units and accompanying activities

The previous section illustrates only some of the possibilities for using early adolescent literature in the middle school. The intent of this section is to provide a framework for developing additional units. With the vast number of early adolescent fiction books available and the endless possibilities for classroom strategies, additional units could be developed to meet the needs of a variety of students and classrooms.

Process For Constructing Units

The following process could be used to develop additional units and accompanying activities:

Sample Case Study Format

Selecting a Theme: Select a characteristic, a conflict, or a concern of early adolescents.

Selecting an Early Adolescent Novel and Character: Select a book that has a central character between the ages of ten and fourteen who exhibits an early adolescent characteristic.

Writing the Case Study: Compose a narrative that includes the following:

- a description of the social, emotional, physical, and intellectual characteristics of the central character;

- a description of a conflict faced by the early adolescent character;

- a description of the character's attempt to cope with the dilemma;

- a description of how the character solves the conflict.

Accompanying Activities

The accompanying activities should include key questions for discussion and journal writings. These questions should be written in a way that will begin to engage early adolescents in thinking about the dilemma or problem. The purpose of these questions is not to test one's understanding of the story but to generate thought and reactions. The use of these questions should be determined by the individual teacher: group discussions, journal writing, cooperative learning, partnership writing, or other activities that engage students in their own learning are all possibilities.

Explorations and Problem Solving

For each case study, exploratory activities are designed to extend the students' involvement in the issues being addressed. Attempts are made to provide variety in the way children could become involved: art, writing, drama, and other strategies. These activities could be completed individually or in cooperative groups. With each case study, one sample activity is included that poses a problem for students to contemplate and solve. This activity provides students an opportunity to extend thinking and promote decision-making and critical thinking.

Extending The Units

1. Use one of the related books included in the units, or a different one, with the accompanying activities. A number of books with related themes could be used in place of the one used in this monograph. Related books are listed with each unit. In most cases, the same questions could be used.

2. Use more than one case study for a set of accompanying activities in order to compare characters, thus, offering more than one selection for students to read.

3. Vary the questions or write additional questions to accompany the case studies, thus providing options for students.

4. Relate the case studies to specific interdisciplinary and/or subject area units.

5. Select more than one of the case studies included and use them together. For example, one could use *Desire for Peer Acceptance* with *Discovering a Personal Identity.*

6. Expand the themes with additional case studies and activities: Sibling Rivalry, Coping with Change, and other issues related to early adolescent development.

7. Use books and accompanying activities to construct a more in-depth unit of study. Perhaps a study entitled "Change" could be developed in which several of the selections could be used within the unit.

8. Extend the literature to include biographies, historical fiction, and children's original stories.

9. Expand the accompanying activities to offer more options for students.

10. Develop a set of themes appropriate for each grade level in the middle school, along with selected literature and activities. This plan could become a sequential program tailored to specific goals at each grade level.

Additional Unit Themes and Early Adolescent Literature

In order to develop additional units that focus on the concerns of early adolescents, the following list reflects additional related unit themes that could be developed. With each unit theme, additional early adolescent literature could be used. Also, the literature used in Chapter 2 could be re-categorized and included with these suggested themes.

Area I: Understanding Oneself

Independence:
Patricia Clapp: *I'm Deborah Sampson: A Soldier in the War of the Revolution*
Constance Greene: *Getting Nowhere*
Judy Blume: *The One in the Middle is the Green Kangaroo*

Making Choices:
Carol Brink: *Caddie Woodlawn*
Tomie de Paola: *The Legend of the Bluebonnet*
Walter Dean Myers: *It Ain't All for Nothing*

Role Identification:
Beverly Cleary: *Ramona the Pest*
E.L. Konigsburg: *From the Mixed Up Files of Mrs. Basil E. Frankweiler*
Betsy Byars: *Summer of the Swans*

Area II: Understanding Relationships

Cooperation:
> Betsy Byars: *The Cybil War*
> Patricia MacLachlan: *Sarah, Plain and Tall*
> Judy Blume: *Tales of a Fourth Grade Nothing*

Belonging:
> Armstrong Sperry: *Sounder*
> Katherine Paterson: *Jacob Have I Loved*
> Cynthia Voight: *Dicey's Song*

Understanding Adults:
> Betsy Byars: *The Night Swimmers*
> Betsy Byars: *Cracker Jackson*

Uses Of Literature Units In Middle Level Education

The case studies have not been written for any particular school organization or for any *one* particular purpose. Following are a few suggested uses of the units.

Teacher-Based Advisory: The case studies and accompanying activities could serve as a teacher-based advisory activity or program. This plan supports the belief that literature can become an advisory vehicle, thus making strong links between the advisory program and the academic curriculum. This plan would assist schools and teachers in conducting teacher-based advisory in such a way that blends reading, writing, and affective development of children. The school could develop a series of case studies at varied grade levels in the middle school, moving from selected themes at the sixth grade into different themes in grades seven and eight.

Pre-Service Teacher Education: The units could be used in middle level education or child growth and development classes to assist pre-service teachers in developing an understanding of the early adolescent. In addition, the units could become a strategy for methods classes in language arts, reading and social studies.

In-Service Workshops/Programs: The units could offer educators an opportunity to come together to read a common selection and address some of the developmental needs of their students in the school. The same process could be used with new teachers in the school to orient them to the need to understand the developmental characteristics of middle school children. Teams could meet to discuss a book, address a concern within the team, and begin to share ideas about the development of early adolescents.

Parent Education: Often, parents are unaware of some of the issues that confront their children. The units could be used by individual parents or with groups of parents to deepen their understanding of their own children. Activities could also help them become acquainted, at the same time, with some of the rich literature for their own children. This strategy would be a way to bring parents together to address some of these. Also, the units could be used by parents with their own children at home.

Interdisciplinary Instruction: Because literature is inherently interdisciplinary, the units could be integrated across the curriculum. For example, a book on multiculturalism could easily be linked to the social studies curriculum and language arts curriculum in the middle school. Many of the books and accompanying activities could be restructured to provide a slant that will link the discussion questions and activities to concepts and skills in various subjects: main idea, drawing conclusion, decision-making, careers, understanding the human body, history, and others. Interdisciplinary teams may choose to use a book in more than one discipline or select several case studies with a common theme to use in various subjects within the team. Interdisciplinary units, such as Cultural Diversity, could become interdisciplinary unit topics to be developed by the team, using the literature within the units.

Language Arts and/or Recreational Reading: One of the most obvious uses is to use the units as one approach in a language arts class and/or recreational reading class for middle school students. This approach blends the emphasis on reading, writing with the personal development of middle school children. As has been advocated in Nancie Atwell's *In the Middle* (1987), opportunities for students to read, write, and respond to a variety of rich literature should be emphasized in the middle school. Such an approach brings to children an opportunity to experience success by reading the case studies, thus perhaps encouraging and stimulating the desire to read the book individually or as a group.

Reflecting On <u>One's Own</u> Early Adolescent Years

Often, adults forget what it was like to be an early adolescent. These units could assist teachers, administrators, and parents in gaining a clearer understanding of early adolescents if they, themselves, reflect on their own early adolescent years. One or more books could be used along with a set of memory joggers to assist adults in reflecting on their own early adolescent years.

A series of questions that could serve as memory joggers will help adults recall what it was like to be an early adolescent. Below are a few examples of some memory joggers. From the stories and reflections that surface from these questions, one could compose a narrative description of his/her own early adolescent years to compare to those of youth in the nineties.

1. Who were important people in your life during the early adolescent years? Who do you think are the important people in the lives of early adolescents?

2. What are some special skills you feel are exhibited by the early adolescents with whom you work? How do these differ from your own when you were that age?

3. Tell about those moments that seem to please early adolescents. Did you share any of these when you were an early adolescent?

4. What compliments did you receive as an early adolescent?

5. What characteristics do you find acceptable in early adolescents? Did you exhibit these as an early adolescent?

6. What are rules that you find most appropriate for early adolescents? What rules do you remember the most? What affect did they have?

7. Describe common behaviors of early adolescents. Describe your behavior when you were that age?

8. What qualities do you bring out in your students? Did you exhibit these qualities when you were that age?

9. What do you notice most often about early adolescent males? About early adolescent females? What roles do you see being acted out? What were some of your roles as a early adolescent?

10. What do you think most early adolescents think about? Why? What do you recall thinking about as an early adolescent?

11. Look at photographs of your students. What do you see? How do you feel? Do these pictures remind you of yourself as an early adolescent?

12. Create a "brag page" about the early adolescents you know. Compose a "brag page" about you as an early adolescent.

13. What have you said to your early adolescents that you feel made an impression? Why? Compare this to your own early adolescent years.

14. What do you recall about your eating habits, clothing choices, music choices and fears? How do they compare or contrast to early adolescents you know.

15. What have you said to early adolescents that took them by surprise? What surprised you as an early adolescent?

16. What was difficult for you as an early adolescent? What was easy?

17. What do you recall talking about in your home when you were growing up? Who did the talking? What were some of the questions?

18. What are some issues that now concern early adolescents? What were some you faced?

19. Interview relatives to collect what they remember about you as an early adolescent.

20. Look at old photographs and tell the stories contained.

21. List your likes, dislikes, disappointments, honors, and laughters as an early adolescent.

22. What did you read as an early adolescent?

23. Who were your friends? Why did you select them as friends? Did your parents approve?

24. What do you recall doing to "win friends and influence people?"

25. Was there a time when you did not like the way you looked? Why? How did you cope?

26. What were two or three of your early adolescent secrets? Why were they secrets?

27. Who was your support as an early adolescent? Why?

28. What qualities of people brought out the best in you? The worst in you?

29. Look at some artifacts from your youth. What did they reveal about you?

30. What were your requests for presents as an early adolescent?

31. Who do you remember from school? What do you remember about them?

32. When did you remember changing some of your interests? What were they? What caused you to change?

33. Do you remember worrying about what your parents thought? Describe.

34. Name some times you did not please your parents or teachers? What did you think about that then?

35. What were some embarrassing times?

36. Do you recall hiding the truth or your feelings? Describe.

37. Was there anything you recall that was hard for you to accomplish? What? How did you learn to accomplish it finally?

38. How would you describe your emotions as an early adolescent?

39. What do you remember learning when you were an early adolescent?

40. Rank order a list of items that you feel were most important to you as an early adolescent.

Conclusion

Schools have come to realize that a developmentally appropriate curriculum for middle level students must go beyond the traditional disciplines of math, science, social studies, and language arts. In order for our youth to become what they can and to become individuals who value themselves and others, schools must realize the significance of a strong affective education program. In fact, like the books written about early adolescents, curriculum should no longer be seen as separate disciplines, each with a unique set of goals that are detached. A curriculum that is tailored to the early adolescent blends affective and intellectual development. Schools continue to struggle with questions concerning how to address both the academic and the affective. Strong teacher-based advisory programs have made their mark. Yet what has often been overlooked are numerous avenues to bridge the academic and the affective within the core courses. As has been the mission of this monograph, efforts could be made to turn to additional resources through which to deepen our understanding of early adolescents. Literature offers one avenue for this. By the time this monograph is published, many new early adolescent books will have surfaced. The process of examining early adolescent literature is an endless task. A practice that could expand this monograph is to involve young adolescents in recommending additional books. They can offer us valuable information about how to help them become continuous learners. They have a sense of what is relevant for them.

Bibliography of Selected Early Adolescent Literature

Babbitt, Natalie. (1975). *Tuck Everlasting*. New York: Farrar, Straus, Giroux.

Bauer, Marion. (1977). *Foster Child*. Minneapolis, Minnesota: The Seabury Press, Inc.

Benjamin, Carol. (1982). *The Wicked Stepdog*. New York: Crowell-Collier Press.

Blume, Judy. (1970). *Are You There God? It's Me, Margaret*. New York: E.P. Dutton.

_____. (1974). *Blubber*. New York: Bradbury Press.

_____. (1971). *Deenie*. New York: Bradbury Press.

_____. (1972). *Tales of a Fourth Grade Nothing*. New York: E.P. Dutton.

_____. (1981). *The One in the Middle is the Green Kangaroo*. New York: Bradbury Press.

_____. (1971). *Then Again, Maybe I Won't*. New York: Bradbury Press.

_____. (1981) *Tiger Eyes*. New York: Bradbury Press.

Bridgers, Sue Ellen. (1957). *Home Before Dark*. New York: Random House.

Brink, Carol. (1973). *Caddie Woodlawn*. New York: Macmillan Publishing Co.

Burch, Robert. (1966). *Queenie Peavy*. New York: Viking Penguin, Inc.

Byars, Betsy. (1974). *After the Goat Man*. New York: Viking Penguin, Inc.

_____. (1985). *Craacker Jackson*. New York: Viking Penguin, Inc.

_____. (1970). *Summer of the Swans*. New York: Viking Penguin, Inc.

_____. (1982). *The Animal, Vegetable and John D. Jones*. New York: Delacorte Press.

_____. (1981). *The Cybil War*. New York: Viking Penguin, Inc.

_____. (1980). *The Night Swimmers*. New York: Delacorte Press.

Clapp, Patricia. (1977). *I'm Deborah Sampson: A Soldier in the War of the Revolution*. New York: Lothrop, Lee and Shepard.

Cleary, Beverly. (1983). *Dear Mr. Henshaw*. New York: William Morrow and Company, Inc.

_____. (1977). *Ramona and Her Father*. New York: William Morrow and Company, Inc.

_____. (1968). *Romona the Pest*. New York: William Morrow and Company, Inc.

Cleaver, Vera and Bill. (1973). *Me Too*. Philadelphia, Pennsylvania: J.B. Lippincott Co.

_____. (1978). *Queen of Hearts*. Philadelphia, Pennsylvania: J.B. Lippincott Co.

_____. (1969). *Where the Lilies Bloom*. Philadephia, Pennsylvania: J.B. Lippincott Co.

Cleaver, Vera. (1985) *Sweetly Sings the Donkey*. New York: Harper and Row, Publishers.

Crane, Stephen. (1962). *The Red Badge of Courage*. New York: Norton.

Cunningham, Julia. (1970). *Burnish Me Bright*. New York: Pantheon Books, Inc.

Danzinger, Paula. (1979). *Can You Sue Your Parents for Malpractice?* New York: Delacorte Press.

_____. (1978). *The Pistachio Prescription*. New York: Delacorte Press.

DeClements, Barthe. (1981). *Nothing's Fair in Fifth Grade*. New York: Viking Press.

dePaola, Tomie. (1973). *Nana Upstairs, Nana Downstairs*. New York: G.P. Putnam Sons.

_____. (1983). *The Legend of the Bluebonnet*. New York: G. P. Putnam Sons.

Duncan, Lois. (1978). *Killing Mr. Griffin*. Boston, Massachusetts: Little, Brown and Co.

Flourney, Valerie. (1985). *The Patchwork Quilt*. New York: Dial Books for Young Readers.

Fox, Paula. (1984). *One-Eyed Cat*. New York: Bradbury Press.

Fritz, Jean. (1987). *The Cabin Faced West*. New York: Puffin Books.

George, Jean Craighead. (1972). *Julie of the Wolves*. New York: Harper and Row,

Publishers.

————. (1959). *My Side of the Mountain*. New York: E.P. Dutton.

————, (1983). *The Talking Earth*. New York: Harper and Row, Publishers.

Goble, Paul. (1978). *The Girl Who Loved Wild Horses*. New York: Bradbury Press.

Goodrich, Frances and Albert Hackett. (1956). *The Diary of Anne Frank*. New York: Houghton Mifflin.

Greene, Bette. (1976) *Beat the Turtle Drum*. New York: Viking Press.

————. (1974). *Philip Hall Likes Me. I Reckon Maybe*. New York: Dial Press.

————. (1973). *Summer of My German Soldier*. New York: Dial Press.

Greene, Constance. (1977) *Getting Nowhere*. New York: Viking Penguin, Inc.

————. (1974). *The Ears of Louis*. New York: Viking Penguin, Inc.

————. (1972). *The Unmaking of Rabbit*. New York: Viking Penguin, Inc.

Haley, Alex. (1976). *Roots*. New York: Doubleday.

Hamilton, Virginia. (1971). *The Planet of Junior Brown*. New York: Macmillan Publishing Co.

————. (1967). *Zeely*. New York: Macmillan Publishing Co.

Klein, Norma. (1972). *Mom, The Wolfman and Me.*. New York: Pantheon Books, Inc.

Konigsburg, E.L. (1967). *From the Mixed Up Files of Mrs. Basil E. Frankweiler*. New York: Anthenum Publishers.

Little, Jean. (1968). *Take Wing*. Boston, Massachusetts: Little, Brown and Co.

Lowry, Lois. (1979). *Anastasia Krupnik*. Boston, Massachusetts: Houghton Mifflin.

————. (1982). *Thirteen Ways to Sink a Sub*. New York: Lothrop, Lee and Shepard.

MacLachlan, Patricia. (1985). *Sarah, Plain and Tall*. New York: Harper and Row, Publishers.

Mann, Peggy. (1973). *My Dad Lives in a Downtown Hotel*. New York: Doubleday and Co., Inc.

————. (1977). *There are Two Kinds of Terrible*. New York: Doubleday and Co., Inc.

Myers, Walter Dean. (1978). *It Ain't All for Nothing*. New York: Viking Penguin, Inc.

O'Dell Scott. (1960). *Island of the Blue Dolphins*. Boston, Massachusetts: Houghton Mifflin, Co.

_____. (1976). *Zia*. Boston, Massachusetts: Houghton Mifflin, Co.

Paterson, Katherine. (1977). *Bridge to Terabithia*. New York: Crowell-Collier Press.

_____. (1985). *Come Sing, Jimmy Jo*. New York: Crowell-Collier Press.

_____. (1980). *Jacob Have I Loved*. New York: Crowell-Collier Press.

Paulsen, Gary. (1985). *Dogsong*. New York: Bradbury Press.

_____. (1987). *Hatchet*. New York: Bradbury Press.

_____. (1984). *Tracker*. New York: Scholastic.

_____. (1990). *Woodsong*. New York: Bradbury Press.

Peck, Richard. (1985). *Remembering the Good Times*. New York: Delacorte Press.

Pfeiffer, Susan Beth. (1981). *What Do You Do When Your Mouth Won't Open?* New York: Delacorte Press.

Rawls, Wilson. (1987). *Where the Red Fern Grows*. Santa Barbara, California: ABC-CLIO.

Seabrooke, Brenda. (1980). *Home Is Where They Take You In*. New York: William Morrow and Company, Inc.

Smith, Doris Buchanan. (1973). *A Taste of Blackberries*. New York: Crowell-Collier Press.

_____. (1975). *Kelly's Creek*. New York: Crowell-Collier Press.

Smith, Robert Kimmel. (1984). *The War with Grandpa*. New York: Delacorte Press.

Speare, Elizabeth. (1983). *Sign of the Beaver*. Boston, Massachusetts: Houghton Mifflin.

Sperry, Armstrong. (1969). *Sounder*. New York: Harper and Row, Publishers.

Spinelli, Jerry. (1990). *Maniac Magee*. Boston, Massachusetts: Little, Brown and Co.

Taylor, Mildred. (1976). *Roll of Thunder, Hear My Cry*. New York: Dial Pess.

Voight, Cynthia. (1982). *Dicey's Song*. New York: Atheneum Publishers.

Yep, Lawrence. (1975). *Dragonwings*. New York: Scholastic.

References

Arnold, John. (1985). A responsive curriculum for early adolescents. *Middle School Journal, 16* (May), 14-18.

Atwell, Nancie. (1987). *In the middle: Writing, reading, and learning with adolescents.* Portsmouth, New Hampshire: Heinemann.

Beane, James A. (1990). *A middle school curriculum From rhetoric to reality.* Columbus, Ohio: National Middle School Association.

Carnegie Council on Adolescent Development. (1989). *Turning points: Preparing American youth for the 21st century.* New York: Carnegie Corporation.

Elkind, David. (1981). *The hurried child.* Reading, Massachusetts: Addison-Wesley Publishing Company.

Hillman, Stephen B. (1991). What developmental psychology has to say about the early adolescent. *Middle School Journal, 23* (September), 3-8.

Probst, Robert. (1984). *Adolescent literature: Response and analysis.* Columbus, Ohio: Charles E. Merrill Publishing Company.

Stevenson, Chris. (1992). *Teaching ten to fourteen year olds.* White Plains, New York: Longman.

Wood, Karen D. and Avett, Susan G. (1993). Bookalogues: Talking About Children's Literature, *Language Arts, 70* (January), 60-65.